WRITING ROMANCE

WRITING ROMANCE

Vanessa Grant

Self-Counsel Press
(a division of)
International Self-Counsel Press Ltd.
Canada   U.S.A.

Printed in Canada

First edition: March 1997; Reprinted: October 1997, January 1999

Canadian Cataloguing in Publication Data

Grant, Vanessa.
　　Writing Romance

　　(Self-counsel writing series)
　　Includes index.
　　ISBN 1-55180-096-9
　　1. Love stories — Authorship.　I. Title.　II. Series
PN3377.5.L68G72 1997　　　　808.3′85　　　C97-910048-8

Cover photography by Terry Guscott, ATN Visuals, Vancouver, B.C.

Self-Counsel Press
(a division of)
International Self-Counsel Press Ltd.

1704 N. State Street
Bellingham, WA 98225

1481 Charlotte Road
North Vancouver, BC V7J 1H1

Contents

Samples

Preface

The love relationship between a man and a woman is one of the most important in adult life. Because it's so crucial to our lives, romantic love features in almost all our fiction, and in ballads, poetry, movies, and dreams. Half of all paperbacks sold are romance novels, stories in which hero and heroine struggle to overcome the obstacles to romantic love. Because people care about love, they want to read about it, and they want to write about it.

I read the chaste romances of the 1950s as a lonely child, fantasizing a romantic hero who would cherish me. I fantasized myself writing a romance novel, too, and when a virus kept me in bed for a month at the age of 12, I started writing my first love story. It foundered on page 50, but I never forgot the excitement of bringing characters to life.

I grew up, married, and had children, but the urge to write never left. I read everything — romances, mysteries, and science fiction. I fantasized different endings to the books I read, and whenever I couldn't find anything good to read, the urge to write my own book would return.

I wrote three unpublished novels while living on a lighthouse station when my children were babies. After leaving the lighthouse, I wrote articles for local newspapers and regional magazines, then commentaries for the CBC [Canadian Broadcasting Corporation] radio. Because that didn't pay well, I became an accountant and a college instructor, but still fantasized myself as a novelist.

Finally, writing nights in 1983 while teaching business at a community college, I wrote *Pacific Disturbance* and sold the completed manuscript to Harlequin Books in 1984. My career as a romance writer had begun!

When I was asked to lead a weekend workshop for beginning writers in 1990, I discovered how rewarding it is to share what I've learned with others who also dream of writing about love. I accepted more speaking engagements, lecturing on topics from characterization to pacing, from goal setting to conflict, rewarded by the enthusiasm of developing writers with eager questions.

I accumulated a filing cabinet full of lecture notes and a growing realization that it was time to organize these notes into a book. By the time Ruth Wilson of Self-Counsel Press suggested I write this book, I was eager to start the project.

Have you ever thought about writing a love story? Have you ever read a romance novel and wondered if you could write one? Do you have a story you want to tell, but don't know how to begin? Have you ever wondered if a newcomer can break into the romance market?

In this book, I try to answer the questions developing writers have asked me over the last six years. What makes a successful love story? What does a successful romance need? Are there any no-no's? How and when should you write about sensuality? When can you break the rules? Is it okay to write about controversial issues? Where do ideas come from?

I discuss how you can use your own fears and dreams as story resources. I look at the process of getting from idea to finished novel, and at characters, motivation, conflict, tension, and plot. I talk about keeping track of details, what to do if you get stuck, how to develop power in your writing, and how to market your finished romance.

This book has been enriched by a number of people I want to thank. Romance writers Daphne Clair, Carole Dean, Robyn Donald, Kate Frieman, Judy Griffith Gill, Grace Green, Naomi Horton, and Kathi Webb contributed items which appear in some of the figures and samples. Literary agent Carolyn Swayze contributed "An Agent's Ideal Writer," and I also want to thank her for being my ideal literary agent. Katherine Orr, vice-president of public relations at Harlequin Enterprises, contributed current Harlequin and Silhouette guidelines and permission to reprint them. Ruth Wilson, managing editor at Self-Counsel Press, contributed enthusiasm and perceptive suggestions, the best gifts an editor can give a writer. Most of all, my husband Brian contributed 20 years of love, support, and belief in my dreams.

Because over 95% of romance readers are women and the romance genre is primarily women's literature, I've often used the female

pronoun in this book to refer to readers of romance. It's important for romance writers to realize they are writing primarily for women. For romantic fantasy to be successful in a novel, it must empower its women readers by affirming values of love and relationship.

Ask yourself why you want to write romance. Is it for the money? Is it because you want to see your name on the bookshelves? Or is it because you're excited by the thought of having characters and love come to life under your fingers as you type on your keyboard? Are you choosing to write romance because half of all books published are romances, or because you believe in love? Above all, published romance writers believe in the power of romantic love.

Read a lot of romances. Ask yourself what makes each one exciting, romantic, or fulfilling. Watch how people behave when they're in love. Look for the problems that make happy-ever-after difficult for lovers. Read this book, then begin writing your own romance.

Part 1

Planning your romance novel

1.

Ingredients of a successful romance novel

a. Category or single-title?

Romance novels can be divided into two types according to how they are published: category romances and single-title romances.

1. Category romances

Category romances are marketed monthly under imprints readers have learned to associate with romance — Harlequin Presents, Bantam Loveswept, Silhouette Special Edition. Each book bearing the same imprint carries a distinctive cover design its readers recognize. Under each imprint or "line," the publisher issues a fixed number of titles each month. To reduce costs, all books in the line have a fixed page length. Once printed, they are marketed in a block. Each store selling the line agrees to accept a fixed quantity of each title monthly. In addition, many category romance lines are also marketed by publisher book clubs.

Readers have certain expectations of category romances: they will be romantic, they will have a happy ending, and the theme will be empowering.

When a new writer sells to a category market, she has the advantage that the book will be delivered to every drugstore, grocery store, and bookstore selling her category line, and also to book club subscribers. Because of this large exposure, the new writer may earn good money writing her first category romance. As her name becomes better known, readers will also recognize her name on the shelves and she can hope sales will increase. (For more information about specific categories and their publishers, see Appendix 2.)

2. Single-title romances

Single-title romance novels are not part of a category line, their page length is not fixed, and each is sold on an individual basis. The reader must examine the book spine or title page to identify the publisher or imprint. Avon, Bantam, Berkley/Jove, Dell, Harlequin Mira, Harper Paperbacks, Kensington Publishing Corp., Penguin Books, Pocket Books, Leisure Books, St. Martin's Press, and Warner Books all publish single-title romances.

An author's income is generally based on royalties paid as a percentage of the cover price of books sold. Because booksellers order single-title books by author and title, a single-title novel is a gamble for a new writer. If the publisher pushes the book, the booksellers stock it, and readers buy it, a single-title novel may do very well. As with category romance, the single-title author's sales may increase as she writes more books and readers come to identify her books as a good read.

3. Your romance novel

Whether you choose category romance or single-title romance depends on the type of story you like reading and the area of the market you feel comfortable tackling. Whichever area of the market you choose as your goal, you'll want to write a successful romantic story that excites both you and your readers.

b. Ingredients of a successful romance

1. A story question

A good novel begins by stirring a question in the reader's mind: the "story question." The nature of your story question is determined by the type of novel you are writing. In a romance novel, the story question is usually something like: Will the heroine overcome her problems and find true love and partnership? The story question must remain the focus throughout the story, and should never be completely answered until the end of the novel.

> A good novel begins by stirring a question in the reader's mind.

2. An empowering story

The best love stories are fantasies in which the deep emotional values of love, family, and partnership in marriage emerge victorious over

4

lesser values. Even when the ending is unhappy, the value of love triumphs, as in the bestselling romance *Bridges of Madison County* and the classic movie *Casablanca*. Hero and heroine are deeply altered by their love. They emerge from their struggles more emotionally whole than they began.

3. A sympathetic heroine

The reader wants to identify with the heroine, care about her, and believe in her. The heroine need not be beautiful, but it must be believable that the hero finds her attractive. Many memorable romances have been written about heroines with disabilities. In *Draw Down the Moon*, Bobby Hutchinson told the story of a heroine bound by a wheelchair. In *Mermaid*, Judy Griffith Gill created a courageous yet vulnerable heroine with only one leg. Whether physically whole or disabled, your heroine needs strong personality characteristics and at least one believable and non-trivial weakness. She needs fears, dreams, hopes, a personal history, and hang-ups. She should begin the story at a change or crisis point in her life. Depending on the category of fiction you choose, she could be any adult age.

4. A hero she can love

Your hero must be a man your heroine can love. Although the stereotypical hero is strong, macho, taciturn, and stubborn, many memorable romances have featured unique heroes who do not fit this profile. Like the heroine, your hero needs strengths, weaknesses, goals, and dreams. He should also begin the story at a change or crisis point in his life. Depending on the category you are writing for, he may be either older or younger than the heroine.

5. An interesting initial conflict or problem

Most good books begin with an immediate initial problem or conflict which keeps the reader turning pages until the core conflict develops. By the time the immediate problem is solved, other problems have developed. Although this initial conflict rarely has the emotional depth to carry the book, it should be related to the characters and the core conflict.

6. An emotionally intense core conflict

As your hero and heroine come to know each other, new obstacles to their happy ending must appear, or the original conflict must grow and change. In the strongest stories, the developing conflict grows out of the characters of hero and heroine to reveal a core difficulty between them which must be resolved before they can have a successful relationship.

7. A plot

To be interesting, the events in your romance novel must be important to your characters. In a successful romance novel, the story or plot develops logically and naturally from character and conflict.

8. Appropriate sensuality

In a successful romance novel, the degree of sexual intimacy must be appropriate to the characters and the story. A love scene should reveal hero and heroine's feelings and the excitement of their growing intimacy. The most powerful love scenes are ones in which the writer focuses on the emotions of the characters, not the clinical details of lovemaking.

9. Archetypes

Throughout time, certain character types appear again and again in our myths and stories, based on patterns or archetypes. Psychologist Carl Jung believed many powerful archetypes have a deep universal appeal.

If you have a strong story idea that you care about passionately, it probably contains at least one powerful archetype. To develop an awareness of archetypes you might use in your stories, think about the themes and characters you like reading about. Look at the descriptions of archetypes on the next page and ask yourself if the characters that touch you fit any archetypes.

10. Black moment and satisfying resolution

As you read a good novel, the obstacles to happiness and fulfillment intensify as the story progresses. As you near the end of the book, you reach a point where it seems impossible for hero and heroine to resolve their differences. This is the black moment.

The more emotionally intense a black moment is, the more satisfying the reader will find the resolution and victory that follows. A particularly intense black moment is created when a character experiences the event he or she most fears. For example, the heroine who fears abandonment may discover the hero has abandoned and betrayed her.

Wild woman — She's passionately and completely herself. She's certain of her identity, of who and what she is. She never needs to wear a mask or pretend to be someone she is not.

Angry young man — He sees injustices all around him, and his life is consumed with the need to rage at these injustices, to do battle against them.

Hero/Heroine devoted to a cause — "The cause" is so important that everything else must be sacrificed to it. Friendships, ambitions, love relationships, possessions must all be given up for the cause.

Passionate artist — The artist is consumed by the need to create. Everything that happens in the artist's life becomes grist for the mill of art. The artist might suffer deeply at the death of a friend, but at the same time will probably soon need to put that suffering into a painting, a novel, a poem, a song. He or she is able to love deeply but cannot give up art.

Weary warrior — The weary warrior is usually a man. He has done battle, has seen death, and become drained by it. A deeply moral man, he has become cynical about his own ability to right wrongs. He is usually placed in a story where he must once again do battle, must come out of his withdrawal and take up his sword. He is seen in many stories of burned-out cops, weary secret agents, crusaders returning embittered from the battles.

Earth mother — Earth mother has a bottomless well of maternal love to give. She nurtures simply by being there. She is well grounded, seems unshakable. She is fulfilled by giving to babies, husbands, friends, who all come away from her arms strengthened. Her strength is quiet and certain.

Virginal heroine — She feels deeply, cares deeply about those around her, but shies away from intimacy with men, sensing a danger she can't define. She is unconscious of her own deeply passionate nature until awakened by the hero.

Alpha hero — See Robyn Donald's description of the Alpha hero below.

11. An emotionally satisfying ending

When readers pick up a category romance, they expect a happy ending. In a single-title romance, a happy ending isn't strictly necessary, although most single-title romances do have a happy ending. Whether the ending is happy or sad, by the time hero and heroine arrive at the end, they must achieve personal growth. The ending must be emotionally satisfying, affirming the values of love and positive relationships.

Robyn Donald on... The Alpha Hero

Why is your hero so tough, hard and outrageously masculine? You need to know, so that you understand what sent him down the Alpha road. What secret vulnerability is he hiding — especially from the heroine? An Alpha hero should directly threaten the heroine's peace of mind, her way of life, but never forget — he's a good man.

Show that he's a hero, with all that that implies — generosity of spirit, competence, confidence. Because he's a hero, he is never needlessly rude or aggressive.

A hero demands high standards. Although he's a natural leader, that inborn authority and control over his emotions have been honed by intelligence, experience, and circumstances. The writer needs to know what those circumstances were, or discover them as she writes.

An Alpha hero tries to behave according to his own ideas of honor. If he fails, he has an over-riding reason for his treachery — often the greater good of mankind — for which he may feel he has to sacrifice both his own happiness and that of the heroine.

There's an aura of danger about the Alpha hero. This man lives by his own rules; he's strong-willed enough to impose those rules on others, but he has a healthy respect for humanity and its laws.

At first he may not understand that the strong sexual attraction he feels for the heroine can be transmuted into love. He may begin by being cynical about emotions, but by the end of the book he's learned that he can trust the heroine with his happiness and honor. So he must have the capacity to love, to feel compassion, to learn to live with another person.

c. *Can a successful romance deal with controversial issues?*

Thirty years ago, category publishers would seldom buy a novel that dealt with a controversial issue. Today, the extent to which a romance editor will be friendly toward a book dealing with a sensitive issue depends on the editor's interests and the publisher's recent experiences.

Here are only a few of the issues that have been tackled in category romance:

- **Harlequin Presents:** In Daphne Clair's *Marriage Under Fire*, a heroine re-examining her life and her marriage commits adultery against the hero. In *No Escape*, Daphne Clair's heroine has abandoned the daughter she loves because she's afraid of physically abusing her.

- **Harlequin Superromance:** In *Every Move You Make*, Bobby Hutchinson's heroine is stalked by a man she once dated. In Judith Duncan's *Streets of Fire*, an ex-prostitute and an injured ex-policeman struggle to find their happy ending.

- **Silhouette Special Edition:** In *An Interrupted Marriage*, Laurey Bright tells the story of a heroine who has spent two years in a mental hospital. In *Phoenix Rising*, Mary Kirk's heroine kidnaps her son from his abusive father and goes on the run to protect him. In *Embers*, Mary Kirk's heroine returns to the childhood home where she was an incest victim. In *Miracles*, Mary Kirk's hero has recovered from a near-death experience only to find he's now a psychic healer.

If you are writing about a controversial issue, watch the bookshelves carefully to discover which publishers and which lines are dealing with similar issues today.

d. *Your own romance novel*

Because each area of the romance genre has its own unique flavor, there's probably a place for your story idea somewhere in the genre. For the best chance of publication, study market information before writing and submitting your story. Read what's being published today, and read about writing and about romance. For more resources, see Appendixes 2 and 3.

Ingredients of a Successful Romance

1. Opens with a question that stirs the reader's mind.
2. Is empowering, affirming the values of love, family, and relationship.
3. Has a sympathetic heroine the reader can care about.
4. Has a hero both the heroine and the reader can fall in love with.
5. Begins with an interesting initial conflict or problem.
6. Develops an emotionally intense core conflict.
7. Keeps hero, heroine, and reader involved in continuing complications and problems for the characters — the plot.
8. Has a level of sensuality appropriate to the characters and the story.
9. Contains at least one powerful character type the reader will recognize and identify with — an archetype.
10. Develops to a black moment when all seems lost.
11. Concludes with an ending that affirms the values of love and positive relationships, and satisfies the reader.

9

Daphne Clair on... Controversial Issues in Romance Novels

Serious matters are dealt with successfully in romance by being individualized, given a personal face. One woman's efforts to overcome the effects of rape on her love life, or one man's battle with alcoholism for the sake of his relationship with a woman, described by a skilled and sincere writer, can illuminate, educate, comfort and influence, even mobilize. A reader who cares about your characters will gain understanding of their problems in a wider sense. Stories influence readers.

"Big" issues like saving whales or rain forests tend to overwhelm the story. If the heroine has reared a pet whale from birth, or lives in the threatened rain forest, there's a germ of a story — not about whales or rain forests but about two people. Does the sheltered but imprisoned whale represent the heroine's own need for security? Or does the hero's determination to build a road and hospital in the wilds arise from guilt at failing to save his son from some tropical disease? And how does that affect the love story?

The issue should be central, not an extra that could be removed without affecting the romance. But a romance is not about a problem. It is about a woman or a man with a specific problem who falls in love with someone who at first compounds the problem and ultimately helps resolve it. The relationship between two people falling in love is at the heart of every romance.

2.

Beginning your story

a. *The story spark —*
where do ideas come from?

Story ideas come from life, from the subconscious, from the creative part of the brain. Your stories can be sparked by things you hear, things that happen, by your own stray thoughts.

1. *Writing about your fears*

When you fear something, your fear generates "what-if" thoughts: What if the plane crashes? What if the dog bites? What if those boys are a gang of muggers? The spark that starts you wondering "what if" can provide the driving force for your novel.

Try dumping your character into your worst nightmare.

My novel *Wild Passage* was sparked by a terrifying sailing experience. My husband and I were en route from British Columbia to San Francisco in our 46-foot sailboat when we were caught in a nighttime gale. While Brian was on deck reducing sail, I lost control of the steering and the boom swept across the deck with a massive crash. When I lost sight of Brian, I was terrified he'd been struck by the boom.

A moment later I spotted him, safe on the foredeck, but the aftereffects of my fear left me tormented by my own fantasies. What if I'm out here and he gets killed, swept overboard in a gale? It's dark, there's a storm, no help except on the other end of a radio. Can I handle it? Will I crumble in a mass of terror?

I created the heroine of *Wild Passage* from my own uncomfortable fantasies. Serena, the heroine, thought she wanted to go sailing, then discovered she was scared witless when she got to sea. I put her through the gale I'd experienced, then left her alone in the storm with an unconscious hero, in control of a 46-foot sailboat. Serena was terrified, but she coped. She grew stronger as she triumphed over fear.

Are you afraid of something? Try dumping your character into your worst nightmare.

2. Myths and fairy tales

Myths, fairy tales, and archetypes provide wonderful story sparks. The fairy tale *Cinderella* has been written again and again in romance: handsome hero falls in love with sweet, hardworking heroine and gives her the love, happiness, and wealth she truly deserves.

3. Reversing stereotypes

In several of my books, I've reversed a stereotype to create my story. The single stay-at-home mom is a stereotypical image. What about a single stay-at-home dad, like my hero Lyle in *Stray Lady?* We usually think of a "rolling stone" as a man. What about a heroine who can't settle down, like Lyle's heroine Georgina?

4. Eternal favorites

Some situations are eternal favorites among both romance readers and writers.

- **The lovers reunited book** — Hero and heroine were once lovers, but something went wrong with the relationship. The story opens with them meeting again. This time, more mature, they face and conquer the issues that separated them in the past.

- **The hidden baby book** — This is a special case of the lovers reunited story. Hero and heroine have an affair, or perhaps even marry. After they separate, the heroine discovers she's pregnant. When the hero reappears in her life, he discovers she's hidden his child from him. In the modern hidden baby story, the heroine needs a good reason for concealing the pregnancy and birth from the father. Of my 25 books, two have used the hidden baby plot device: *Hidden Memories* and *Yesterday's Vows.*

- **The amnesia book** — The heroine or hero who has amnesia has a special conflict. How can anyone enter into a new relationship not knowing if there is a spouse waiting, forgotten behind the barrier of memory? Most prolific authors have either written an amnesia book or have one they'd like to write.

- **The kidnap book** — The hero kidnaps the heroine, often for the sake of family honor. Forced into close quarters, they fall in love. Since kidnapping is a criminal offense, and male abuse of physical power is widely disapproved of today, the kidnapping must be exceptionally well motivated, as it is in Robyn Donald's *Tiger Eyes.*

- **The woman in jeopardy book** — Mary Higgins Clark and Joy Fielding have made careers out of this plot, and many romance novels feature it. The heroine is in danger, usually from an unclear source. She doesn't know who her enemy is, she may even think she's imagining the danger. The hero may appear to be the enemy.

b. What if...

Stories come in many different ways, but once the spark comes into a storyteller's mind, the next step is to ask "What if ...?" The following is an example of how my story *So Much for Dreams* grew.

In 1988, Brian and I were living in Mexico. While he stayed in the tropics to watch over our sailboat, I traveled north to Arizona with friends to purchase a used car. My friends and I returned a week later, driving my newly acquired Oldsmobile south through the mountains in steaming weather. When the Oldsmobile overheated and we had to nurse it down the Baja peninsula, I felt quite safe. I spoke Spanish, I knew the helpful good-nature of the Mexican people, and I had friends with me.

But what if a woman were driving these mountain roads in an undependable car, unable to speak Spanish, not knowing the country? What if her car broke down in one of these remote mountains? Driving an undependable car alone in a remote area of a country where you don't speak the language is a dangerous thing to do. If my fictional heroine were to do such a stupid thing, she needed a good reason to put herself at risk.

Perhaps she worked with young girls in trouble. Maybe one of her young charges had disappeared into Mexico. What if my heroine — I'll call her Dinah — got a letter from this young girl who is pregnant, abandoned, living on the beach in La Paz, Mexico? She couldn't call the girl, there's no phone.

Around this time, I heard from a writer friend who had received a battered letter from me in her mail, mysteriously delivered months after I sent it.

Once a story spark comes into your mind, ask yourself, "What if...?"

What if Dinah's young friend sent her letter weeks before Dinah got it?

I decided Dinah was actively helping young girls, that she'd come out of a traumatic childhood strong and involved in life. In contrast, I gave her a hero who had responded to trauma by withdrawing from the world. I made Joe a drifter, living on his sailboat in Mexico, hiding from the pain of his past, with no intention of ever becoming involved again.

I began *So Much for Dreams* with Dinah driving her aging Oldsmobile up a Mexican mountain. I tossed Joe in her path and gave them a reason to travel together. By the time the initial problems of Dinah's car and her pregnant young friend were resolved, Joe and Dinah were facing a deeper conflict — her committed life versus his vow never to risk caring again.

c. Getting ideas

How do you come up with ideas?

- List ten places you've been.
- List ten things you've done.
- List ten things you'd like to do.
- List ten personal problems you have trouble dealing with.
- List ten things you fear.
- List ten things you feel guilty about.

You've got a lifetime of story material here — settings, occupations, events, motivations. Look at your fears. Could you use one to spark a story? What's your favorite holiday location? Put a heroine in that location, give her one of your problems, and ask yourself, what if...?

3.

Character-driven plotting

For my first few books, I wrote detailed plots before beginning to write the novel. In every case, I found myself struggling with awkward scenes and stubborn characters. By my fifth book, I realized much of the planning for my books happens outside my conscious mind. I began working more on character development, and I learned to trust my characters to develop the story in their own way. As I stopped playing God with my characters, writing became easier and more pleasurable, and my books got better.

a. The character-driven story

- *African Queen:* It's a story about two people who make an epic journey through Africa on a beat-up boat.

- *The Bridges of Madison County:* It's a story about an artistic, wandering photographer with no emotional ties, who falls in love with a passionate woman trapped in a conventional rural life.

- *Love Story:* It's a story about a woman who falls in love, gets married, then dies of cancer.

- *Romancing the Stone:* It's a story about an introverted woman who learns her sister is in trouble in South America and goes to help despite her fear of jungles and life.

Classic love stories. No matter how I describe each of them, I can't say more than a few words before I come to the heart of the story — its people.

Authors can and do play God, deliberately dumping characters into uncomfortable situations, but it is the characters themselves who control each powerful story, the characters who chose how to react when faced with the crises their authors create.

Joan Wilder, the heroine of *Romancing the Stone*, fears jungles, bugs, and life. The author dumps Joan into an impossible situation, giving her a choice between abandoning her sister to die and facing the South American jungle.

That's the essence of character-driven plotting in romance: take a strongly developed heroine and dump her in an uncomfortable situation with a unique hero, then see what happens.

b. Character free will

Fictional characters write their own stories.

Within the limits of the world the author creates, each memorable character has free will. Like living people, fictional characters write their own stories by reacting to events, making decisions consistent with their personalities and history. If the heroine of *Romancing the Stone* had been hardheaded and unromantic, confident and aggressive, it would have been a different story. By her own nature, Joan Wilder shaped her story.

c. The plot-character relationship: how it works

Stories are born in many different ways. Writers read something, see something, overhear something...and the storyteller begins to wonder "what if?"

The original spark for my romance novel *Taking Chances* came when I read a novel in which the hero kidnapped the heroine for family reasons. I didn't believe in the hero's motivation, and I couldn't believe the heroine would fall in love with this man. In disgust, I vowed I'd write a story in which the heroine kidnaps the hero. I titled the idea *Kidnap* and began playing with it.

1. The people

The story spark for Shakespeare's *Hamlet* might well have been the question: What if a man encountered his father's ghost and learned that his father had been murdered? If Shakespeare asked that question, he must immediately have followed it with others: What kind of man was the son? What about the ghost? The murderer? Did the son have a wife? A girlfriend? A mother? A pet dog? Friends? What were his relationships to these other people? Was he a fighter? A bookworm? What were his dreams, his goals, his hang-ups? Until those questions were answered, Shakespeare would not have been able to tell Hamlet's story.

What if a woman kidnapped a man?

Before I could go further, I needed to answer many questions. Why would she kidnap him? Who is she? Who are the people around her? What are her hopes, dreams, goals? What is she afraid of? What does she believe she's best at? Worst? What makes her comfortable? Uncomfortable?

I couldn't begin telling the story until I knew both hero and heroine intimately. I also needed to know where they lived and what effect their setting had on them.

I decided to set the story in British Columbia, using the logging industry as a background. I created brothers and cousins, a family business, and a heroine related to the hero by marriage. After several days, I had a lot of notes and a dead idea. On the surface my story looked okay, but despite the kidnapping and loving, and complications, I didn't have a plot.

2. Where does plot come from?

Characters are people with history, hang-ups, and goals. People interact with each other and with their environment, generating events. Put the events together and when it works, you have a plot, a story.

Kidnap wasn't working. My characters weren't willing to go through with the kidnapping. They thought it was stupid and melodramatic, but the idea kept nagging at me.

3. Impatience

Up to this point, I'd spent very little time thinking about my heroine's character. I'd given her a name — Misty — but I didn't know if she had a dog or not, or whether she ate eggs for breakfast. I wanted to get on with my story.

The reader may never care about the dusty details of Misty's history. I may never tell the reader where she was born or whether she failed high school French. The only person who is certain to care is Misty herself. Like all characters, she has the potential to turn into a stubborn witch if I ignore her dreams and fears. If I pile up a

Requirements for Plot Germination

The author needs —

- A story spark plus living characters

Living characters need —

- Personality
- Abilities and disabilities
- History, hang-ups, and goals
- Relationships to career, house, city, weather, traffic, etc.
- Relationships (past and present) to friends, family, lovers, and pets
- An attitude to love and marriage

The story needs —

- A plot goal (i.e., hero and heroine achieve true partnership)
- An opening conflict or problem to get things started
- Living characters with goals, forced to face a difficult situation
- Obstacles between characters and their goals
- A setting, complete with characters' attitudes to the setting

The most important rule: Everything is disposable!

breathless series of disasters for Misty without stopping to find out what she wants, I'll suddenly discover that she's become a bull-headed hunk of cardboard — or a rebellious teenager.

I wrote the first two chapters and completed many pages of plotting notes, but none of it worked. I had a family logging business, a kidnapping to keep the hero from a meeting, a handful of other details, and a dead story.

4. Believing in your story

I wanted Misty to become an assertive, exciting heroine, to fall in love with an exciting, strong hero. I gave her exciting acts to perform, kidnapping and love, but she moved through my story with the animation of a tin soldier! I couldn't believe in her motivation for kidnapping the hero. I had no idea why they should fall in love.

Misty was a cardboard character, and I couldn't make her come to life, so I put *Kidnap* aside, hoping one day I'd find a way to use the idea. I stored my notes and the first two chapters in a directory called IDEAS on my computer's hard drive.

d. Breathing life into the story spark

I still wanted to write the story. I liked the idea of the hero kidnapped by the heroine to keep him from a business meeting, but I needed the right characters to make this story work. While I waited for inspiration, I worked on *Wild Passage*.

I wrote *Wild Passage* while Brian and I were berthed at the visitor's dock of the San Diego Yacht Club. Late at night, we would go up to the hot pool and Jacuzzi and laze about in unaccustomed luxury, staring up at the stars and a big palm tree at one end of the pool.

I decided to give the hero of *Wild Passage* an older brother named Zeb, the sort of man everybody turns to when in trouble. While writing Zeb's brief scene in *Wild Passage*, I realized he was the perfect hero for *Kidnap*.

I had a setting, too: San Diego and the Yacht Club, that pool in the middle of a solitary night. I made my fictional pool part of a privately owned marina for rich yacht owners, made my hero and his family owners of the marina and associated shipyard. I decided Zeb lived in a big, ornate house next door to the marina and every night at midnight, he came for a solitary swim in the pool. He was a creature of habit.

When I started grooming Zeb for the job of hero, I decided he would have another brother, a twin, who wanted to keep him away from the shareholders' meeting of the family corporation. This twin brother would trick a private detective into kidnapping Zeb.

The detective would be my heroine.

e. Breathing life into the hero

There are two steps to breathing life into a character. First, formulate a basic personality description of the character. Second, flesh out the skeleton with relationships and roles.

1. Personality and development

I wanted the hero to be a man accustomed to looking after everyone but himself: a man who secretly yearns for excitement in his life, but can't have it because he's too busy being responsible for those around him. From these requirements, I developed the personality description (see Sample #1).

Next, I outlined Zeb's base characteristics, placing him in terms of age, physical appearance, and culture. In making up these characteristics, I wrote whatever I felt fit his basic personality. I then created the significant events in his past. These details, added to Zeb's basic cultural background, must explain how he became the person he is. Why is Zeb the one who looks after the rest of the family? Why does he yearn for adventure instead of taking it? I created a man groomed as a child to be family caretaker.

2. Relationships and roles

A man behaves differently to his sister than his secretary. Basic personality, beliefs, and emotions determine how these roles are played. Looking at how my hero behaves in all his relationships enables me to understand how he will behave in my novel.

I defined Zeb by the roles in his life as shown in Sample #2. Although some of these details never got into the book, I needed them to know Zeb intimately and write about him without hesitation.

Sample #1
Hero's Personality and Development

PERSONALITY	Zebadiah John Turner is solid, dependable, tends to keep to a routine, a gentle, caring man who is not easily pushed around. Although he is successful, he secretly yearns for excitement in his life. (I plan to give him some!)

BASICS	**BASE CHARACTERISTICS**
Birth	Born San Diego 40 years ago. Son of prominent San Diego shipyard owner
Race/culture	White, Anglo-Saxon Protestant
Religion at birth	Methodist
Physical	Tidy brown medium-length hair, hazel eyes, six feet tall, broad shoulders, lean body with hidden strength

DEVELOPMENT	*SIGNIFICANT FACTORS AND EVENTS*
Parental training	1. Brought up wealthy and groomed to take over family responsibilities.
Education	2. Oldest of three boys, father sheltered his wife, and Zeb learned to do the same.
Occupation	3. Took over management of family business when father died. Zeb was 20, quit college to take over.
Social	4. Took in his younger brother's son last year when brother having trouble with the kid.
	5. Never married. He isn't sure why. Too busy looking after the dependents he has.
	6. Life has always been serious for Zeb.

PERSONALITY	Zebadiah John Turner is solid, dependable, tends to keep to a routine, a gentle caring man who is not easily pushed around. Although he is successful, he secretly yearns for excitement in his life.
RELATIONSHIPS	**ROLES**
Parents	**Mother** — Zeb looks after her, bails her out of problems with resigned patience. He does not expect her to think for herself. **Father** (deceased) — Zeb looks after the business and the dependents his father left him.
Siblings	**Barry** (Zeb's twin, younger, divorced from his wife) is always in trouble. Zeb makes sure the wife and child Barry abandoned are okay (i.e., looks after Barry's responsibilities). **Neil** (2 yrs. younger) Zeb feels protective urges toward younger brother, but Neil will seldom accept, and usually does not need, help. However, Zeb is making a home for Neil's son at present.
Nephews	**Keith** (Neil's son) is living with Zeb. Zeb takes time to be buddies with the boy, has a good relationship that's pretty loose. **Justin** (Barry's son). Zeb keeps a watchful eye on him, because Barry doesn't.
Lover	**Alice** — she's another person who leans on him. No excitement, just habit. They've known each other all their lives. She asks his advice in business. From her he gets nothing but safe sex and another emotional dependent.
Sister-in-law	**Helen** — Calls Zeb whenever Barry's alimony check is late, or Justin needs glasses.
Family business	**Shipyard and marina** — run efficiently by Zeb. As a result, the whole family is getting richer in a conservative way.
Employees	**Marina guard** — Zeb keeps up on news about the man's family, new baby.
His name	**Zebadiah John** — He could dodge his unusual name by using John, but he doesn't. Doesn't dodge responsibility either.
Church	Attends weddings, funerals, and family occasions.

f. Next comes the heroine

Because Zeb was conventional, I wanted an unconventional heroine. Because he was accustomed to dependents, he needed a heroine who'd never been looked after. She was tough, capable, independent. Zeb secretly wanted excitement, so I gave him Misty, a woman designed to shake him out of his sedate rut (see Sample #3).

1. Personality and development

I designed Misty to create an inherent conflict between hero and heroine. I began with her personality, creating her in contrast to Zeb. Where he was secure in personal and family relationships, but a stranger to adventure, I made her comfortable with danger, but uncomfortable in personal relationships.

I decided Misty was a white Anglo-Saxon Protestant also, giving hero and heroine a common cultural heritage. But while I'd given Zeb a physical appearance consistent with his personality, I made Misty a small, blonde woman people tended to label as "fluffy" rather than the intelligent and talented woman she was.

Nothing in Misty's basic origins explained how she became a private detective comfortable with danger and subterfuge, yet wary of personal relationships. The answer must lie in the events of her development. I decided that while Zeb knew everything about his past and his family, Misty knew almost nothing.

I know from studying psychology that trauma and abandonment in the formative first six years of life may be impossible to overcome, so I gave Misty a loving and secure home for the first six years of her life. I followed Misty's early security with a tragic accident that killed her parents, putting her into the care of her alcoholic, private-detective uncle. Misty's unconventional childhood taught her not to rely on anyone. Her childhood apprenticeship in a detective agency reinforced her ability to look after herself.

When I decided Misty didn't know how her parents had died, I realized they had been killed in a car accident and that Uncle Kenny had been driving. This family secret provided mystery in Misty's background, and also reinforced her adult role as a professional who specialized in finding out things people have hidden. I decided Misty had never used her profession to find out what happened to her parents. She was afraid to find out, sensing her knowledge could destroy her relationship with her only relative.

Sample #3
Heroine's Personality and Development

PERSONALITY	Misty Donovan is intelligent and adventurous, enjoys danger and a challenge. Confident in her job as a private detective, but insecure in personal relationships. Does not trust anyone to look after her, depends on her own judgment and resents being pushed around. She's shattered when anything happens to people she cares about — knows how to handle other people's crises, not her own.

BASICS	**BASE CHARACTERISTICS**
Birth	Born in northern United States 26 years ago.
Race/culture	Middle class white Anglo-Saxon Protestant.
Religion at birth	she doesn't know
Physical	Five feet, two inches tall, small, slender, not voluptuous although feminine looking. Strong slender muscles, fit. Blonde hair, naturally curly. People often mistake her for a fluffy blonde, a fact she uses in her work and believes she's learned not to resent.

DEVELOPMENT	**SIGNIFICANT FACTORS AND EVENTS**
Parental training *Education* *Occupation* *Social*	1. Brought up well-loved until around age 5 or 6 when she was orphaned. She doesn't know what happened to parents; her uncle who took her in charge never explained. 2. Sent to boarding schools, summers in uncle's bachelor pad. At 8, she asked uncle what happened to parents. He stormed out on a drunken bender and did not return for a week. She learned not to trust and kept money stashed to feed herself if he disappeared again. 3. From 8, she spent most of her holidays hanging around the detective agency her uncle owned. She became skillful at following people, etc. 4. She went to college, fell in love with a wealthy man who dumped her when he realized how unsuitable her background was (i.e., when he met uncle Kenny). 5. She went to work for her uncle, became his partner, and now looks after him.

Sample #4
Heroine's Relationships and Roles

PERSONALITY	Misty Donovan is intelligent and adventurous, enjoys danger and a challenge. Confident in her job as a private detective, but insecure in personal relationships. Does not trust anyone to look after her, depends on her own judgment and resents being pushed around. She's shattered when anything happens to people she cares about — knows how to handle other people's crises, not her own.
RELATIONSHIPS	*ROLES*
Parents	**Died early in her life.** Misty doesn't know how, is afraid to ask Uncle Kenny after one attempt when she was 8.
Siblings	**None**
Uncle	**Kenny** — Misty loves him but does not trust him. She works to please him, knows she's more important to him as a partner in the business than as a niece. She's afraid to ask questions or she might lose him and he's the only relative she has. She ignores his benders and covers for him.
Family business	**Detective agency** — She learned it from Kenny, but now she's the one who keeps it going. She's good at pretend games and sleuthing.
Employees	**Jo-Anne** — Misty and Kenny's secretary. They work more as partners than boss and employee. Joanne is an old-timer who knows the score, secretly loves Kenny, and wants romance for Misty.
Lovers	**Wayne** — she fell in love with him, did everything she could to be what he wanted, to play the right role, but it wasn't enough. She knows better now than to try to fit where she doesn't belong.
Car	A white Corvette she loves, fast and exciting.
Dog	**Max** — a vicious-looking Doberman she rescued when he was abandoned. Max barks at shadows and paper bags, and gives Misty the only unconditional love she has. Max is probably the only being Misty truly trusts. She bought her house to give the dog a home.

2. Relationships and roles

Because Misty's development was so unconventional, the relationships and roles in her life were more unusual than Zeb's (see Sample #4).

The most important relationship in Misty's present life is with Uncle Kenny. She cares about him deeply, but fears losing him if she makes demands of him. This insecure relationship provides the background for Misty's other relationships and the explanation for both her discomfort in personal relationships and her comfort with dangerous situations.

Since Misty has so few intimate relationships, there's a danger the reader might find her cold and uncaring. To avoid this, I showed her yearning for intimacy by giving her Max, her dog.

g. About motivation

Motivation is an essential part of character development. As I prepare to write a book, I always write notes about characters and their history. As I explore a character's backstory — the events that take place before my book begins — I'm constantly working to understand what motivates this person. Why does Zeb always look after his family? Why hasn't he married? Why doesn't Misty trust anyone to look after her? Why does Kenny get drunk every time Misty asks about her past?

As human beings, our actions and patterns can often be explained by events in our past. Sometimes a single event provides powerful motivation, beginning the pattern of our present behavior. Author Naomi Horton calls an event like this a *prime motivating event.* Once a prime motivating event occurs, subsequent events often reinforce it. A woman whose father abandoned her when she was seven years old might have an issue with abandonment. If she then marries a man who abandons her, her distrust of men in intimate relationships will be reinforced, and in her dealings with men, she'll experience the prime motivating force of distrust.

If your characters' personality and prime motivating forces develop from prime motivating events, your readers will readily understand why they behave as they do.

Misty's prime motivating force is distrust. She learned not to count on people when her parents disappeared without explanation when she was five (prime motivating event.) When she was eight, her uncle reinforced this distrust by disappearing and leaving her

Naomi Horton on...Character Motivation

Motivation is the secret —

- *to great characterization*
- *to great conflict*
- *to great emotional intensity*

Romance novel characters do not just appear in this world fully grown with no history, family, or life. Like real people, they've had things happen to them — good and bad — that affect who they are, what they think, how they see the world, how they react to other people. In short, it's what makes them tick.

Motivation: What makes these people tick?

Your hero and heroine should have one major motivation driving them through your story: this is their prime motivating force (PMF). It will color their every thought and will affect their every move. For the sake of your story, this PMF will have stemmed from a single, dramatic event in the character's past — the prime motivating event (PME).

Create a realistic backstory for both hero and heroine before starting to write your book. To create strong emotional intensity, make the PME and resulting PMF emotionally powerful. To create strong romantic and emotional conflict between hero and heroine, give them conflicting prime motivating forces.

***Example:** You have a hero who is fiercely driven to fight crime (PMF) because his family was murdered when he was a child (PME). That PMF leads him to work as an undercover cop, and he lives by lies — his job is to make criminals trust him, and then he uses that trust to bring them to justice. If you have him meet a heroine whose PMF is the opposite — a woman who hates lies and liars and believes there is never an excuse to lie to someone — you will have emotional conflict. Especially if she discovers that, as part of his job, he's been lying to her. (See* No Lies Between Us, *by Naomi Horton, Silhouette Desire, 1991).*

PMEs and PMFs do not always have to be negative: if a man who was hurt in love and doesn't trust his heart falls in love with a woman whose PME and PMF has taught her there is nothing that the power of love can't heal, they will be in tremendous — and powerful — conflict.

alone for a week. At college, her lover Wayne reinforced her distrust again.

Zeb's prime motivating force is a need to look after people. He was trained to it, then the motivating event of his father's death threw him into his Mr. Responsibility role. All the relationships around him reinforce that role.

h. Putting characters together

Zeb and Misty's characters, histories, hang-ups, and goals make certain things inevitable when they get together.

- Zeb is going to want to look after Misty. It's as natural as breathing to him.
- Misty doesn't trust anyone to look after her.
- This conflict between their goals will cause trouble.
- Once Zeb falls in love, he's going to want marriage and kids.
- Misty knows she can't fit into the world of the wealthy and stuffy. Even Zeb's house frightens her.
- This conflict between their goals will cause more trouble.

I decided to use the title *Taking Chances*, because Zeb avoided taking chances, while Misty was willing to take chances everywhere except in her private life.

As I began writing the story, I returned to my story spark. Zeb's charming brother Barry asks Misty to kidnap Zeb. I began writing the scene, but almost immediately came into conflict with the character I'd created. Misty was nobody's fool. She'd grown up on lies and evasions. No matter how good a con Barry presented, wouldn't she see though him?

Of course she would.

The most important rule: Everything is disposable!

I threw out the kidnapping, but I felt a little tug, my desire to have this man in Misty's physical power. She's a small girl. He's a big man. But once Misty met Zeb and began falling under his spell, I decided there was nothing stopping her from fantasizing about how she would have kidnapped him, if…

Character Checklist

- Do your characters fit the story spark?
- Are they alive? Do you care about them?
- What do these people want?
- Why can't they have it?
- Should they have it?
- What happens when goal meets obstacle?
- What then?
- What doesn't work about this whole thing?

When it doesn't work…
- Throw out the… character…spark…setting.
- Begin again.

4.

More about characters

a. Wounded characters and heavy baggage

You need characters with strong personalities: characters real enough to have both strengths and weaknesses. In developing these characters, you'll give them problems and triumphs and some emotional baggage to carry into the story. In *Taking Chances*, Zeb carried into the story the baggage of a lifetime of responsibilities and a hidden dream of having his own adventure. Misty carried a lifetime of distrust and a secret yearning for a loving home.

Some years ago I began writing a book called *Going Home*, about a woman named Annie who gave up her newborn child for adoption, then ran away to Mexico to live. Annie yearned for her child, for the home she'd never had. Distrustful and wounded, she blocked relationships from her life, except one relationship with a neighboring Mexican boy. In the course of the story, Annie returned to build a relationship with her daughter. She also found love with a hero.

Although everyone who read *Going Home* was moved by Annie and her daughter Jenny, I couldn't find a publisher for the book. It took a perceptive critic to point out that for most of the story Annie is a victim, weighed down by old pain and grief. She was not taking charge of her own life. She was only reacting to the events I'd written for her.

Annie needed to take action. It didn't matter if she made mistakes, but she must be active in determining her own fate. One day, I may try writing Annie's story again. If so, I'll write about a wounded woman whose *actions* provide the catalyst for events in the story.

She'll make mistakes, but she'll win her happy ending with her own strong efforts.

Whatever your characters' baggage, it's important it doesn't weigh them down to the point of being passive. In *Taking Chances,*. Misty is distrustful and Zeb yearns for something different, but both are active, making decisions. If Misty were so distrustful of others that she couldn't even fantasize a relationship with Zeb, it would be hard to write the romance.

b. Your best friends as characters

Your best friend's name is Constance and you want to write her into your romance novel. The idea excites you, and of course Constance will be thrilled.

Don't do it!

Pick up your favorite romance novel. Turn to the page after the cover page and read the notice to the effect that, "All the characters in this book have no existence outside the imagination of the author, and have no relation whatsoever to anyone bearing the same name or names. They are not even distantly inspired by any individual known or unknown to the author..."

When you submit a novel to a publisher, the publisher expects you have written what belongs to you, your **imaginary** story. If the publisher knew Constance was your best friend, you'd never get a contract for the book. The publisher wouldn't risk a possible lawsuit.

Even if the publisher would never find out, even if Constance wouldn't sue, don't do it.

As you develop your conflict, the hero you thought was a harsh man may show a gentle side when he's with children, dogs, and the heroine. The heroine you thought good-natured may be enraged when the hero doesn't give her the promotion she was certain she'd earned. Inevitably, if you've created strong, believable characters in a real-life conflict, those characters will surprise you. They'll change and shift, and as a writer your job will be to watch and try to understand the changes, and respond by being willing to redraw your characters when needed.

Because Constance is your friend, she's not going to change with the needs of the story. If you use her, she'll limit how powerful your story can become. You'll always be aware that one day she'll read what you've written.

> Whatever your characters' baggage, it's important that it doesn't weigh them down to the point of making them passive.

As a writer, you can't afford to worry about what your characters think of you.

c. *Using real people creatively*

You can't afford to worry about what your characters think of you.

You may look at Constance and see a beautiful, talented woman who is inexplicably alone. Your writer's mind plays with the situation. What if a beautiful woman, happily living alone, one day met a man who made her yearn for romance and marriage?

To develop this story, you must leave Constance behind. You must ask, "Why is she alone? Why hasn't she had a serious relationship before?" Perhaps she has. When she finds herself attracted to the hero, what stops her from reaching for him? What if he's the image of the con man who romanced her out of her savings 15 years ago?

Without Constance looking over your shoulder, you're free to follow this heroine wherever your questions lead. The resulting character will be unlikely to have any resemblance to Constance. She's the product of your imagination, sparked by the question "What if…?"

d. *Techniques for getting to know your characters*

You have some concept of your hero and heroine, but to write a real page-turner, you must know your characters intimately. What motivates these people? How can you flesh them out into real people? Your heroine is determined never to fall under the hero's spell again. Why?

Sometimes characters' motivations and histories emerge full grown in our minds. At other times, it seems a curtain hides our characters from us. How can you pull that curtain aside?

1. *The character journal*

Naomi Horton once told me she'd had a problem with her hero, so she sat down and let him tell her the answer — writing in first person. I borrowed her technique some time later when I was developing my first thriller, *Right of Darkness*.

My hero had taken to the road with his motorcycle. I knew he was running from something. I knew he would meet my heroine and something about her would force him to stop, to take part in life. Everything hinged on what had happened to the hero in New Jersey.

But whenever I asked myself, "What happened in New Jersey?" the answers seemed artificial, stilted, and unbelievable.

I sat down at my computer, opened a new, empty file, and began writing. I told myself it didn't matter what I wrote, this wasn't part of the book, just a file I could delete later. I began by writing, "My name is Devin…" and I forced my fingers to keep typing although I had nothing to say.

> *My name is Devin. I had a regular woman once. That was a long time ago. Another life. I'm not going back, there's nothing to go back for. The myths have exploded.*

As I typed, Devin's past came to life for me. I understood what he was running from, why he couldn't go back. Somehow, putting myself into the first person, actually typing "My name is Devin…" got me into his skin in a way my usual techniques couldn't.

2. *The character interview*

Romance author Carole Dean uses a character interview technique for getting to the bottom of reticent characters. For the interview, you need a tape recorder and a friend willing to play the role of a reporter asking probing questions. The results can be both astounding and inspiring.

Carole Dean on… The Character Interview

Characters are the heartbeat of our stories, but for most of us our heroes and heroines don't jump, fully formed, into chapter 1. We have to create them — with a past logical enough to make their romantic present believable and compelling. The character interview can help. It's effective — and fun.

The idea is to become the character in your book, get inside his or her head and stay there until the character's fictional actions and reactions are as true as a carpenter's plumb line. How?

1. *Ask a friend to be your interviewer. A writer friend is best; he or she will understand what you're trying to do.*

2. *Record the interview. Recording will eliminate the distraction of taking notes.*

3. *Give your interviewer a starter list of questions, then tell him or her to wing it, ask anything at all.*

4. *Slip into character and answer all questions in the first person.*

Here's a small sample:

- *Where and when were you born?*
- *Tell me about your parents.*
- *Was your family rich, poor, or middle class? How did this affect you?*
- *Which parent were you closest to? What's your relationship today?*
- *Any siblings? Tell me about them. What's your relationship today?*
- *What's your educational background?*
- *Did you like school? If not, why not?*
- *Did you have a pet?*
- *Ever been married? What happened?*
- *What do you consider your best physical feature?*
- *Do you read? What kind of reading? Books? Magazines? Newspapers?*
- *What makes you angry?*
- *What do you care about most?*

5.

Conflict and struggle

a. Conflict is a struggle

Whenever your characters struggle, they experience conflict. Characters, and human beings, experience both internal and external conflict.

1. Internal conflict

Internal conflict is a *person's internal struggle* over opposing goals. It's inside, hidden from witnesses. Your characters need internal conflict.

In *Hidden Memories,* my heroine Abby has a secret. Everyone believes her daughter Trish is her dead husband's child. Only Abby knows Trish was conceived as the result of a couple of hours spent with Ryan, a man she let pick her up when she was in shock after her husband's death. Abby pretends Trish is her husband Ben's child, but the lie causes an internal struggle. She knows she should be honest about her daughter's origins, yet her fear of what the truth will do to her relationships with her parents, her daughter, her daughter's grandfather, and the world stops her from revealing the truth.

Abby wants to be an honest person. She also wants to hide the truth about her daughter's birth. Because she can't have both, she experiences an internal struggle between these two opposing goals.

Although Abby has struggled with her lie for years, at the opening of my story the conflict over how she should behave remains hidden inside her. She's been able to keep this internal conflict at a manageable level by telling herself no one will gain if she tells the truth. She'll only hurt those she loves.

Abby's internal conflict *could* affect everyone around her if she acts: her daughter, her daughter's father, her daughter's grandfather, and her parents.

When a character feeling internal conflict acts out of that struggle, it becomes externalized, creating conflict with other characters.

2. External conflict

External conflict is the *struggle between people* over opposing goals. External conflict is out in the open. It's visible to witnesses.

In *Hidden Memories*, Abby's goal is to keep her secret. When Abby has a transaction with someone who opposes that goal, that's external conflict. When characters with opposing goals have transactions with each other, those transactions must reflect the struggle between them, the external conflict.

Ryan has been obsessed with Abby's memory ever since she disappeared within hours of his first meeting her. When he appears in chapter 1, he unknowingly opposes Abby's goal of keeping her secret.

When Ryan recognizes Abby, he wants to know why she ran away. He wants to be sure she doesn't get away again. Ryan's goal of learning all he can about Abby and his resulting transactions with her threaten her secret further. She fears he'll learn she has a daughter and realize he's the father. Because he threatens Abby's secret, Ryan's appearance in Abby's life creates external conflict.

3. Your characters must experience both internal and external conflict

It takes external conflict to generate excitement.

If your characters don't experience any internal conflict, you're telling the reader the issues in this story aren't important enough to worry about. But internal conflict is not enough. If your heroine never experiences an external threat to her goals, she'll spend the whole book agonizing about her internal struggle.

It takes external conflict to generate excitement.

In *Hidden Memories*, when Abby sees her child's father across a crowded room, she tries to hide from him. Ryan could expose her secret, throw her life into turmoil. Even before she makes the first move in her struggle with Ryan, even before there's any evidence of external conflict between her and Ryan, Abby's level of internal conflict has risen sky high. She's struggling with her conscience, Ryan's right to know his child, and her desire to avoid the unpleasantness that will result if her secret is exposed. Her mind is in turmoil.

What if he finds out about Trish? Can I get out of here before he sees me? Does he know I'm here? What if he finds out? What if he tries to take Trish from me? How can I explain this to my mother? She'll be so disappointed in me. And Trish's grandfather, he'll never forgive me. He'll turn away from Trish.

Ryan and Abby have conflicting goals. Ryan wants to know why Abby disappeared after their brief affair. Once he learns she's had his child, he wants to form a strong relationship with his daughter. Because Abby wants to maintain the fiction that Trish is her dead husband's daughter, Ryan and Abby's opposing goals create conflict.

Every step in the external struggle between Ryan and Abby makes Abby's internal conflict worse. Because of her internal conflict, when the external conflict begins, her reactions are instinctive, not logical. She's under stress, attacked from outside by Ryan, from inside by her own conscience. She tries to hide, to pretend, to evade. Ryan becomes suspicious. Abby's mother likes Ryan and unknowingly makes the situation worse by throwing them together.

With strong internal conflict, and strong interlinking external conflict, the stakes rise. The reader fears it won't work out for these people. Abby may drive Ryan away with her inability to live openly with the truth. Ryan may become angry and leave. The more uncertainty the reader feels over the outcome, the more satisfied she'll be when hero and heroine come together in the end.

> In your story, *external* conflict should always make the internal conflict worse.

> In your story, *internal* conflict should always make the external conflict worse.

b. With Strings Attached

In *With Strings Attached,* my heroine Molly has a lifelong internal struggle concerning her relationship with her father. She loves him, wants to believe he loves her, but past experience tells her he invariably lets her down.

Molly is in conflict with herself each time she thinks about her father. She tells herself she doesn't care about the disappointments, but she does care. She tells herself not to expect anything, but she expects regardless.

When Molly's father gives her a cabin on Gabriola Island, she wants to believe he's showing his love, but fears his gift will have strings attached. She drives to Gabriola Island fighting with herself, trying to bury her hopes under a layer of skepticism. Molly's long-standing internal conflict over her father has been made worse by his gift. Both her hope and her fear have grown.

Molly is also secretly ashamed of her father. He's a womanizer, irresponsible, always doing shocking things. Her shame, her love, and her loyalty for her father create an internal battle. She fears other people's condemnation of her father and believes it will extend to her, yet she feels compelled to protect him. More internal conflict.

When I wrote *With Strings Attached,* I could have tried to write a book in which the main conflict was this: Molly falls in love with Patrick, yet can't trust him because she's been let down so often by her father. She fears Patrick's family will find out her father's faults and judge her by them.

This sort of internal conflict could make it hard for any woman to have a successful relationship, but although internal conflict is necessary to a good story, it's not enough. I need *external* conflict to make the internal conflict worse. I need *internal* conflict to make the external worse.

So I up the stakes. I make Patrick a public figure. When Molly realizes he's being courted by his political party to run for office, she knows a long-term relationship is impossible. Her father's scandals would be disastrous to Patrick. She must choose between her need for Patrick and his welfare: internal conflict. She begins to avoid Patrick, a transaction creating external conflict. He pursues her harder: another external conflict transaction. The closer they come, the worse Molly's internal conflict becomes. To ease her internal conflict, she tries to draw away from Patrick, causing more external conflict between her and Patrick.

I up the stakes again with a couple of transactions between Molly and her father to make Molly suspect a new scandal is about to explode. Molly now has external conflict with her father. She opposes Patrick's pursuit of her more strongly — more external conflict — trying to lesson the impact when everything inevitably blows up.

But Patrick won't stay away, and her father's public scandal explodes. The external conflict — trouble from her father and relationship aggression from Patrick — makes the internal conflict unbearable. Molly runs from her father's mess, her lover, and the new life she craves. Molly's running is an external conflict transaction, a non-verbal message Patrick takes as rejection. He pursues her, and she throws nasty words at him to get free. More external conflict, resulting in both Molly and Patrick being miserable.

The misery is internal. The actions are external.

The internal conflict — Molly's love for her father and fear of his betrayals and scandals — makes the external conflict worse. The external conflict — Patrick's uncomfortable pursuit of Molly despite her need for caution and her father's unfolding current disaster — makes the internal conflict worse.

c. *Conflict of love*

As your story goes on, your conflict must change and develop. Your hero and heroine must have trouble getting what they want, they must worry about it, doubting whether their relationship can work. For good reasons, they must commit offenses against each other. We all commit offenses against the people we love: because we're tired, worried, or feeling afraid we're not loved as much as we love. Those are good emotional reasons arising from our internal conflicts. They generate transactions that are part of external conflict.

Falling in love produces both internal and external conflict. We hurt the people we love. They hurt us. To have a successful relationship, your heroine must became vulnerable to someone she cares about, knowing that person will sometimes hurt her, but trusting the relationship will be worth it.

In a love story, the conflict eventually develops to make the reader ask: "Do these two people care enough about each other to make the compromises necessary? Will they put their relationship above these other problems? Can they trust each other enough to become vulnerable, revealing their inner selves and committing to a lasting relationship the reader can believe in?"

> In acting out their conflict transactions, your hero and heroine will commit offenses against each other.

d. *Opening versus developing conflict*

All good stories begin with some sort of conflict, either internal or external. The conflict at the beginning of your book may or may not be related to the core conflict that unfolds as the story goes on. The opening conflict's real purpose is to keep the reader interested while you as author introduce characters and begin to show the bigger struggle that drives your story. The opening conflict need not be deep, although it may be, but it must feel real and it should tell the reader something about the character on stage.

In *Hidden Memories*, I opened by dumping the reader into the primary conflict of my story, having Abby see the one man in the world who could refute her lie about her daughter's parentage. By the time Ryan discovers Abby's lie, Abby and Ryan are struggling with their own new relationship. The external conflict issues have changed. Now Abby and Ryan are struggling to divide their daughter between them. They're also struggling between Abby's fear of committing to another relationship after her disastrous marriage and Ryan's desire to have a family relationship with both Abby and Trish.

In *With Strings Attached*, I opened with the heroine in a state of internal conflict, rushing to get to the cabin her father gave to her before the cat he abandoned dies of hunger.

Molly's internal conflict isn't as earth shattering as Abby's initial "It couldn't be him!" from *Hidden Memories*. The opening conflict doesn't have to be earth shattering, but it should be immediate. If it's internal conflict, it should quickly lead to external. The reader should feel urgency about turning the page, and the opening conflict should not be resolved until the characters have other immediate problems.

e. Adversity and conflict

Your character may experience adversity — a traffic accident, a plane crash, a best suit rained on, a baby dying. But although adversity may cause severe problems, you also need conflict. Characters are powerless to change adversity, and readers need to know that the character's actions matter.

f. How to create conflict

> To create conflict, first give your character a goal, then have someone oppose that goal.

Conflict is created when goals meet obstacles. To create conflict, first give your character a goal, then have someone oppose that goal.

In *Hidden Memories*, Abby's goal was to keep the secret of her child's birth. Ryan opposed that goal, first discovering her secret, then making it impossible for her to keep it.

In *With Strings Attached*, Molly's goal was to avoid relationships where her father's scandals could hurt her. Patrick opposed that goal by falling in love with her and being a public figure. Her father further opposed that goal by dumping her in a tax evasion scandal.

To create conflict in your novel, give your character a goal with a high level of internal conflict, then have someone oppose that goal.

Goals Stimulate Conflict

Whenever a character has a goal, conflict will result if another character opposes that goal. How hard the characters fight and how strong the conflict is will depend on how high the stakes are.

Factors affecting the degree of conflict:

1. *How much the character desires the goal.* Characters will fight hardest for what they desire most intensely.

2. *How confident the character is of achieving the goal.* If the heroine is confident of getting a promotion, she may be slow to see a threat to her goal. If she fears she won't be selected, she may fight over much smaller signs of opposition or competition.

3. *How flexible the character is about how and when the goal is achieved.* A heroine who wants to sell a novel one day won't fight as hard as one who intensely wants to sell a novel this year.

4. *How much the character will lose in the event of failure.* In *Hidden Memories*, Abby fears she will lose her daughter's love and her family's respect if her secret is exposed. Those are high stakes. For the writer in 3., above, if she's broke the stakes are higher because failing to sell may mean she has her mortgage foreclosed, has to go on welfare, can't put her son through university. The more it matters, the harder she'll fight.

To create conflict in your novel, give your character a goal with a high level of internal conflict, then have someone oppose that goal.

g. Common goals and related conflicts

1. Romantic love

In a romance novel, whether hero and heroine realize it or not, their common goal is to achieve a strong and lasting relationship with each other.

Internal conflict occurs whenever a person forms strong emotional bonds. We all fear betrayal, being hurt, not being lovable enough for the other person. These fears will be present to some degree in both hero and heroine.

External conflict results because any differences between hero and heroine affect their goal of emotional love. In your story, it's important for both hero and heroine to struggle with the external results of their internal conflict regarding the relationship. The heroine may have difficulty letting herself be vulnerable to the hero, trusting he won't carelessly or deliberately hurt her. External conflict will show itself as the opposition between her difficulty in trusting enough to be vulnerable to him, and his pain and anger over evidences of her lack of trust.

2. Keeping or winning possessions

Internal conflict occurs when a character worries about getting or keeping the desired house, car, business, or job, or struggles over whether the sought-after goal is the right one.

External conflict occurs when character A makes it difficult for B to get coveted possessions, or threatens to take what B has. In response to the aggressive external conflict transaction, B must either fight or retreat.

3. Keeping secrets

Internal conflict reveals itself in the guilty struggle between the moral desire for truthfulness and the fear of consequences of revealing the secret.

External conflict occurs when character A knows character B's secret, or does something B fears will expose the secret. B struggles against A's actions, hoping to keep the secret concealed. The more drastic the consequences of exposure, the harder the struggle.

4. Gaining achievements

Internal conflict develops because our sense of self-worth is often tied up in our ability to achieve goals. A heroine who intensely wants to be a romance novelist fears she's not a good enough writer. She fears her family will think she's above herself in trying. She fears her marriage will fail if she earns more money than her husband. Her goal of selling a novel is opposed by other strong goals — the need to keep the emotional support of friends and family and the need to avoid exposing her own inadequacy.

External conflict results when the people around her interfere with her goal. An editor may reject her book. Her husband may say, "If you don't quit spending all your time at that computer and start being a wife again, I'm leaving." If our writer can't stop writing despite these unpleasant transactions, both external and internal conflict grow.

What problems can you foresee for these couples?

1. A woman who grew up an only child yearns for a big family. She falls in love with a man who is one of seven siblings. She loves the family at first, until she's forced to deal with a host of unexpected problems. She's a deeply private person as a result of her solitary upbringing. He's family oriented and believes telling their intimate secrets to his family isn't the same as "telling other people." When he tells his family about the pregnancy she asked him to keep secret for a few weeks, she's furious. He can't understand why. He didn't tell anyone outside the family.

2. An extroverted woman makes a habit of adopting stray dogs and children. She meets a brilliant, socially inept scientist and takes him under her motherly wing. He falls in love with her nurturing qualities, yet resents her "stray dog" motivation for caring about him. (Jane Donnelly's *The Man Outside*)

3. An emotionally repressed man fears deep, uncontrolled passion. He falls passionately in love with a performer who exudes passion with every breath, yet his own feelings for her terrify him. (Vanessa Grant's *Dance of Seduction*)

4. He's a minister. She is an ex-prostitute. He loves her and respects her for the obstacles she's overcome, but he fears his congregation learning the truth about her.

5. He's a macho chauvinist. She's a macho girl with a black belt in judo. He admires her, but disapproves of her. He wishes she'd wear skirts, perfume, and display her femininity.

5. Territory

Internal conflict occurs whenever we establish territory, or worry about what we'll do if someone takes our children, our home, our money, or our self-respect.

External conflict occurs when territory is attacked, or we defend territory in response to real or imagined invasions. (See the next chapter for an exploration of territory as a tool for developing story conflict.)

6. Opposites attract conflict

You can encourage conflict in your story if you choose a hero and heroine who have opposing characteristics. They'll tend to fall into opposition, making your job as a writer easier.

Look around you at the couples you know. You're certain to find a number of examples of the "opposites attract" theory. Now, look closer. Often, the very thing that attracts carries the threat of conflict.

h. Learning to be nasty

> To be a good writer, you must treat your characters terribly.

A satisfying book pits characters against overwhelming odds, then leaves them to fight through disaster after disaster until miraculously, victory is won. Heroine and hero may win battles along the way. They may have a wonderful time on a date. They may laugh, make love, or even get married, but despite their victories the problems keep coming until the reader, even the writer, wonders if they'll survive.

The harder you make life for your characters, the better your readers will like the book. Until you reach the final scene, every transaction must present new problems or new developments to old problems. Forget everything you ever learned about being nice to people. To be a good storyteller, you must treat your characters terribly, throwing their worst fears in their faces. Until the end, you must remain nasty to your characters.

6.

Territory: The bridge between character and conflict

a. Primitive urges and danger buttons

Adam and Eve like to laugh together and sometimes they enjoy snuggling up under the bear fur, but first comes survival, food, and shelter. But once the basics are looked after, Adam and Eve should be able to lie back on their bear rug and look at the stars, wondering if anyone is living on Alpha Centauri.

But if they're discussing the stars when a man-eating tiger comes into their cave, they won't live to give birth to Cain and Abel.

How can Adam and Eve be safe enough to relax when the world is full of danger? By establishing territory and patrolling the borders of that territory. By building a castle and putting a moat around it. A drawbridge. Locks on the doors. A guard dog. Territory.

Every individual has the basic drive to create and maintain a safe place. As writers, we can use that basic drive to change a story spark into a plot.

b. Your territory

When you walk into a room filled with strangers, one of the first things you do is establish territory. You find a chair you feel comfortable taking. You sit in the chair. You put your pen and note pad on the table, take your coat off and drape it over the back of the chair, then settle into position. You're feeling more comfortable now. You've established some degree of control over territory. You make a comment to the woman beside you — establishing allies along your border.

The lecturer speaks for an hour, then there's a break. You walk to the back of the room and pour yourself a cup of coffee. You leave your coat on the chair and your note pad on the table as territory markers.

You return and find someone in your chair.

You don't own the chair, but you've carefully positioned your coat, your pad of paper, and your pen as signals that this is your territory. Usually those signals are respected, but not always.

Someone is in your chair. If you were a rational being you would shrug and move your coat and paper to the next chair. It's only a chair. But you're not rational. You have a genetically programmed urge to create a safe place by claiming and enforcing territory. It doesn't matter that losing custody of the lecture chair has nothing to do with your survival. To the primitive part of your mind, keeping territory secure means safety. Safety means survival. Your internal watchman has pushed a yellow alert button. You feel tension, adrenaline in your bloodstream, the urge to fight or to flee.

"Excuse me," you say, "but that's my chair." Or you run. You pick up your possessions and retreat to the other side of the room. The watchman wants you to do something definite. If you sit in the next chair all that energy will still be there. You'll feel the tension. How dare he? He sat in my chair! Couldn't he see I had my coat on it, my note pad?

Territory disputes are one of the most common forms of conflict in our society. A man shoots another man in a dispute over a parking space. A woman shoots her son in a dispute over a messy room. These insane things have actually happened. My parking space. My house. My territory. My safety.

We all have territory: mental, physical, and emotional walls around us. Each one of us has a subconscious watchman whose job is to warn of danger.

> When your characters feel threatened, they'll fight back, or they'll run.

c. Characters' territory

In developing characters, I search for areas of territorial conflict to germinate my story spark into a plot. When my characters feel threatened, they'll react in one of two ways: they'll fight back, or they'll run.

Looking for a character's territory boundaries, I begin with the character's self-concept. We all have a self-concept that we want to protect, a way we like to look at ourselves. That self-concept has associated territory which must be guarded. If I define my character's self-concept, I'll know his or her psychological territory. If another character violates that territory, I'll have instant conflict.

d. Territorial plot development

A few years ago at a writers' brainstorming session, I shared an idea for a love story involving an Ecuadorian-Canadian archaeologist and a Canadian with a limp she managed to hide. As I explained my vision of the story to this group of writers, I realized the story lacked excitement. There was no conflict between the territories of hero and heroine. They had everything in common, but I doubt they'd fall in love.

Someone suggested using a different heroine, and I asked myself what kind of heroine would fit my archaeologist hero. I understood Ricardo Swan's self-concept. He prided himself on being rational and cool, the result of watching the mismatch between his rational father and his emotional Latin mother. His personal territory forbid him becoming obsessed with anything. Even his love for archaeology was tempered by cool reason.

Using the concept of territory, I knew Ricardo needed a heroine to challenge his self-concept. I decided Ricardo should fall uncomfortably in lust with a sensual, Latin woman, creating an internal struggle between his emotional desires and his rational self-concept.

I decided the heroine would be a performer, a woman in conflict with her own nature. Onstage Maria was a sensual singer and dancer, but the boundaries of her territory as a sensual person were the boundaries of the stage itself. Offstage she was a woman willingly sequestered by her family. Her motivation for this denial of her own passionate nature was a prime motivating event. As a sheltered teenager, she was raped by a teacher she had a crush on. Now she won't allow eligible men to penetrate the borders of her territory.

When I began *Dance of Seduction*, the strong internal conflict of both characters and their incompatible territories immediately drove them into external conflict. Ricardo was forced outside his safe and unemotional territory by his uncomfortable lust for Maria. Unlike the other men Maria had ignored over the years, Ricardo got inside her boundaries to confront her private self. Her watchman sounded

Two people with incompatible territory will always experience conflict.

45
TERRITORY

yellow alert and she used all her normal defenses, but they didn't work because this time Maria undermined her own defenses.

By the time her watchman realized the danger and sounded a red alert, it was too late for Maria to reinforce her borders. She'd already fallen in love with Ricardo.

The moment these two characters broached each other's territory, conflict became inevitable and the story almost wrote itself. In the end, the two characters re-drew their territorial boundaries to make new territory encompassing both.

e. Looking for territorial conflict

Two people with incompatible territory will always experience conflict. For every character you can make up, there's another who will violate that character's territory.

He's a man who wants to save the rain forest. She wants to help him. For this to make a story, the characters need conflict. Perhaps he's a man who's determined to save the rain forest his own way, a man who won't play by the rules. She's a woman who believes in the rules; she even makes some of them. The movie *Medicine Man* is driven by this basic conflict between character territories.

Developing Territorial Conflict

1. Develop character self-concepts and motivations.

2. Describe the areas of territory that each prime character must patrol to maintain his or her self-concept.

3. Determine the most feared dangers from your character's point of view. Normally any red alert danger will be related to some prime motivating event in the character's past.

4. Determine how this character has dealt with territorial invasions in the past. When the watchman pushes the alarm button, the character will normally make a fight or flight choice based on past behavior.

5. The conflict between hero and heroine should have a focus. They need real conflict, real problems. Ask yourself whether there is a natural conflict between territories of hero and heroine.

6. If your characters' territorial boundaries don't show an inherent conflict, you may have trouble developing an interesting plot because of a lack of natural conflict. Look deeper. Look again. Or, like I had to do in *The Dance of Seduction*, recast your story. Get a different hero or heroine.

7. Examine how the territorial habits of hero and heroine will affect each other as their territories cross. This is the essence of your conflict and your plot. This is where problems develop for hero and heroine, where they stop being rational.

7.

Where on earth?

Visit your local bookstore and browse through this month's crop of romance novels. In a typical month you'll find a south sea island or two, several American hometowns, a few New York and San Francisco settings, and a scattering that might include Australia, New Zealand, England, Canada, Japan, and various European settings.

This month's top-selling romance novel could be set anywhere in the world. Your romance novel can also be set anywhere, as long as it's a location that fits the story and one you can write about authentically.

a. What do you need to know about your setting?

1. The atmosphere of your setting

Most important of all, you need to know the atmosphere of your chosen setting. Is it gay and festive like a Mexican city at carnival time? Is it filled with history and tragedy like a Greek ruin? Are the people welcoming, or suspicious? Do they have a laid-back attitude to time, as in many Latin American countries, or are they immersed in rush hours and efficiency?

How isolated is your chosen location from the rest of the world, and what signs of isolation or lack of it are visible to an observer? Are the newspapers two days old? Can a snow slide cut off the population from the outside world? Can you catch a jet to anywhere at the local airport?

What are the sounds, tastes, and smells? You'll want to evoke the flavor of your setting for your readers, and to do so you'll need to understand it yourself.

2. The impact of setting on your characters

How does your chosen location affect the lives of the locals? How will it affect your characters? Your setting may be a background to your story, adding a flavor of realism to your scenes; or it may directly affect the lives of your characters and the outcome of the story.

Here are a few examples of the varying impact of settings from my own books:

- In *Awakening Dreams,* I wrote about a female tax auditor and a male pilot who crashed in the remote wilderness of northern coastal British Columbia. The wilderness setting provided many of my characters' problems: the cold water that could have killed them, the dense bush they had to hike through to find rescue, the local bears. This setting was immediate and life threatening, an essential part of the story.

- In *Angela's Affair,* I wrote about a female canvas worker in Port Townsend, Washington, and a wealthy businessman from Canada. The shipbuilding town provided local color, but the novel could have been set in any North American coastal town without much change to the plot.

- In *Catalina's Lover,* I wrote the story of an American archaeologist and a Peruvian landowner. Because the cultural differences between hero and heroine were one of the biggest problems they had to overcome, the Peruvian setting was a crucial part of the story. This book could not have been set anywhere else without a complete rewrite of the plot and most of the scenes.

After writing over two dozen romance novels, I've come to believe it's easier to write a book with a strong setting, one that affects the lives of the people in my story. I've also noticed that my readers often tell me their favorites are the books in which setting plays a crucial role in the story.

3. How do your characters feel about the setting?

If your characters have strong feelings about the setting, those feelings will give the reader the sensation of being there. If you set your romance in a small town, ask yourself how the heroine feels about the town she lives in. Is it the only home she's ever had, does

It's easier to write a book with a strong setting.

she hate it and yearn for city life? Does the hero find the small-town lack of efficiency irritating or refreshing? Is he indifferent to its charms, or intrigued?

4. What makes your setting exotic?

Wherever you set your novel, the location will be exotic to some readers. If you sell your romance novel to one of the major publishers, it may be sold around the world. Ask yourself what makes your setting unique. That's the thing you want to show your readers. People from far away will find it exotic, and the locals will read it and feel at home.

5. Playing it safe

If you're planning to set your story in a location you've visited but haven't lived in, play it safe by making your main character a stranger to the location.

In the late 1980s I lived in Mexico for two years. Although I've set several books in Mexico, in most of them I've made the characters non-Mexican nationals. Although I have a good feel for the country and its people, I know I don't think like a Mexican national.

When I began writing *The Dance of Seduction,* I realized my heroine had to be a Mexican singer. To explain any inadvertent "Americanisms," I decided Maria had been sent to Los Angeles for her high school education. Similarly, when I wrote *Catalina's Lover,* I had my Peruvian hero educated in England and the United States and gave him an additional seven years living and working outside Peru to explain any non-Latin speech or behavior.

b. Writing about setting

Cynthia Dyson-Paige was still rehearsing what she would say to Jonathan Halley. She'd been practicing the words for hours.

I thought you'd want to help Allan. He needs help...

As you read the passage above, you probably assumed Cynthia to be a woman, but was she indoors? Outdoors? In Africa? New York?

A reader needs a sense of place when reading a novel, a mental image to act as backdrop for the action. If your reader is to be transported into your fictional world, she must be able to make a picture of it. As a writer, it's your job to make it easy for the reader to make mental pictures of your words.

> A reader needs a sense of place when reading a novel.

Here's the same passage as I actually wrote it in my book, *The Moon Lady's Lover*:

> *When the jet landed in Vancouver, Cynthia Dyson-Paige was still rehearsing what she would say to Jonathan Halley. She'd been practicing the words all through the four-hour flight from Toronto.*
>
> *She rented a car at the airport, wincing as her credit card went through the imprinting machine. Then she crawled into Vancouver with the morning rush-hour traffic, still rehearsing the encounter to come.*
>
> *I thought you'd want to help Allan. He needs help…*

With the details I've given, the reader knows Cynthia just disembarked from a jet airplane. The reader has just enough information to make a picture of Cynthia and her surroundings. I can assume most readers are familiar with jets, credit cards, and rush-hour traffic either from their own experience or from movies and other books, so I didn't waste words describing these things.

When I wrote *With Strings Attached*, I began with the heroine Molly coming to a small island on the west coast of Canada. Because few of my readers would be familiar with the complex details of travel from the mainland to the Gulf Islands, I gave details. To avoid boring the reader with a travelogue, I filtered these details into Molly's thoughts and actions.

> *Molly swung the steering wheel to the left and followed a green car through a controlled intersection. Had she just turned on to the Trans-Canada highway? These British Columbians had a nerve, calling it the Trans-Canada highway after interrupting it for a ferry crossing of Georgia Strait. Where the devil were the signs? Could you turn off Route One to that other ferry? Or — Gabriola Island. It must be an Indian name. Or was it Spanish? Gabriola. Yes, Spanish.*
>
> *She knew so little about it. A gulf island nestled against Vancouver Island…*

As you're planning your book, make a note of things about the setting that interest you and plan to weave them into your story.

In describing setting, the emotions evoked are more important than the physical details. A stormy day can be used to foreshadow an emotional storm in the characters. A sunny day may contrast with the violence of a terrible argument.

Guidelines for Setting

1. Determine what your chosen setting feels like to locals and strangers.

2. Define the impact of your setting on your characters. Will isolation affect your story? Will cultural characteristics contribute to your conflict?

3. Is your setting the background for your story, or an essential factor? The answer will determine how much space you give to describing the impact of setting on your characters. The more impact setting has on your characters, the more memorable your readers will find it.

4. How do your characters feel about the setting? Strong feelings about the setting will make it seem more real.

5. If you're writing about a setting you don't know intimately, play it safe by making your character a stranger to the setting.

6. Determine what makes your setting exotic to outsiders, and include these details in your description.

7. Make a note of things about the setting that interest you. What interests you may also interest the reader.

8. Remember to give your reader what she needs to form a mental picture of each scene.

8.

Planning and plotting

You know your characters' hopes, dreams, and fears. You understand the conflict that will drive your story. You know where you'll set your book and how much the location will affect the destiny of the characters. What else do you need before you put your notes aside and start writing?

Some published writers begin writing without much idea of where the story is going, what will happen, or even who the characters are. For them, the characters' actions are a constant surprise as the book goes on. Other writers know every detail before chapter 1 begins. Their characters seldom surprise them.

Most of us fall somewhere between those two extremes.

As you write, you'll find the level of advance planning that's comfortable for you. I'd recommend starting somewhere in the middle. Know your characters, understand what conflicts they will deal with in the course of the book, know your setting and the level of sensuality you intend for the book, then write by stimulus and response.

When I plan a book, it's most important for me to work out motivations, characters, and conflict before I start writing. The plot looks after itself if I've done this groundwork. The odd time I've tried writing a detailed plot outline ahead of time, I've felt trapped by it and often missed signals my characters were giving me.

"I have planned and found the plan a straight jacket, leading to a boring book; not planned and fallen into a black hole. Some books need a plan, others don't. I wish I could predict which they are."

— *Daphne Clair, Harlequin Mills & Boon and Harlequin Presents*

"I don't outline. I live in hope...that my characters will arrive with enough emotional 'luggage' to form a story."

— *Carole Dean, Meteor Kismet and Kensington*

"For me, writing a novel is a journey, full of surprises. When I begin I start with an idea...often for a character, sometimes a vivid image of a scene, sometimes a place or a house, occasionally a source of tension... and I go on from there. I don't outline. I do rewrite a lot."

— *Robyn Donald, Harlequin Mills & Boon and Harlequin Presents*

"I do a tentative 'outline' using 5 x 8 index cards, one per scene, starting with the scenes I know will occur: meeting, first kiss, discovery of conflict, other kisses, love scenes, black moment, resolution. I brainstorm other scenes, keeping my notes very loose, using them as springboards to the writing, and to help my memory. And I change whatever seems to need changing, as I write."

— *Kate Frieman, Silhouette Special Editions and Berkley/Jove Haunting Hearts.*

"No, I don't write from an outline. When I do, it kills the story."

— *Judy Griffith Gill, Bantam Loveswept and Harlequin Love & Laughter*

"I do a character outline and backstory for my characters, not a plot outline. I know the conflict and have a general image of the structure of the story before I start. The story evolves as I write."

— *Naomi Horton, Silhouette Intimate Moments and Silhouette Desire*

a. Plotting by stimulus and response

One of the best descriptions of the process of plotting or planning a novel I've ever read is in Jack M. Bickham's *Writing Novels that Sell*. Bickham reminds us that most actions take place in response to some event or action, and that stimulus and response transactions are the driving force of our stories.

When you're planning what comes next in your story, think about stimulus and response.

When my heroine in *When Love Returns* backs her car out her driveway into the path of the hero's dump truck, David rushes to her car after the accident and finds Julie at the wheel.

- **Stimulus for David:** Julie is alive and conscious, but in unknown condition.

- **Response:** "Can you move? Does it hurt to breathe?"

- **Stimulus for Julie:** Shock of crash, David's appearance and question.

- **Response** (internal): She's nauseous, feels guilty because the accident was her fault.

- **Stimulus for David:** Julie appears unharmed, but David's fear and panic have produced adrenaline that now transforms to anger.

- **Response:** Shouts: "I could have killed you. I damned near did…One day you'll kill yourself with your nonsense!"

- **Stimulus for Julie:** David's shouting.

- **Response:** Defensive. "I didn't stop to think —," provides stimulus for David.

- **Response:** "Damn it, Julie! Do you ever think?"

With stimulus and response, Julie and David have moved from a collision of vehicles into an argument that brings up old frustrations from their past.

You know your characters. You know their goals, dreams, and fears. Before you can finish your novel, you'll need to know the story goal, where you plan to have your characters end. In your romance novel, the story goal is probably something like, "Jack and Jean will overcome their difficulties and achieve a loving partnership." You'll also need a mental picture of how your story starts, for example, "Julie backs down the drive into the path of David's dump truck."

Start with the beginning and build your story with a series of stimulus and response transactions. When something happens, think about how the characters will react to that stimulus. What will Julie do when David accuses her of recklessness? She'll remember the times he bossed her around when she was a kid, her frustration because he never took her seriously. Because she knows she caused the accident but wants him to think well of her, she'll be defensive. If he keeps up the attack, she'll become angry.

When something happens, think about how your characters will react.

Is it realistic for David to shout at Julie moments after hitting her car with his truck? Yes, he's shaken from the accident, can't get rid of the horror of thinking he killed her. He turns on her in the same way we do when we fear a loved one has been hurt, only to find the person was carelessly late.

When your character does something, always ask yourself if there was an appropriate stimulus for the character's action. Will the reader be aware of the stimulus? If not, she won't be able to make sense of your character's behavior. If David had walked over to Julie and shouted, "Damn it, Julie! Do you ever think?" without the provocation of the accident, my readers would be confused and wouldn't believe in David.

There must be a stimulus before each action by your characters.

Everything your characters do must be well motivated. There must be a stimulus before each action. That stimulus may come from the character's own thoughts, from the actions of other characters, or from external events.

Pick up your favorite romance novel and begin re-reading it. Stop at each action and see if you can find the stimulus for that action. You'll probably find the novel is one long chain of stimulus-response transactions.

b. Diagram of a plot

As readers, we've come to expect a certain pattern in a novel. The story begins with our introduction to a character at a turning point or crisis point. This character has a goal or objective, but as the novel progresses obstacles appear to make achieving the goal more difficult. The character struggles, winning battles along the way, but more difficulties appear. Sometimes it seems the character may win, but victory slips away until finally a point comes when all seems lost and victory impossible. This is the climax or black moment of the story. Following the black moment, the character makes a sacrifice to gain a victory.

Love always requires a sacrifice.

This pattern of fiction has been alive since the time of the Greek tragedies. Characters struggle, obstacles mount up, all seems lost. Finally, a victory is won, but always at a cost. Perhaps the reason for the eternal popularity of love stories is that all human beings understand that the intimacy of love has a personal cost. We can love only by allowing ourselves to become vulnerable to another person, by giving up our right to sole determination of our futures. Love always requires a sacrifice.

Part 2

Ready, set, go!
What you need to get there

9.

About computers

a. Do you need a computer?

If you dislike computers, feel nervous of them, or believe you can't afford one, I urge you to reconsider. Even the most basic and primitive computer — the sort people often give away because it's outdated — will give you freedom from retyping your work every time you need to make a change. In addition, most publishers' contracts have a standard clause requiring the writer to provide a copy of the manuscript on computer disk. (This electronic copy of the manuscript is requested after the publisher decides to buy the book. Don't send it when you first submit your novel to a publisher.)

b. Capturing inspiration

Lying in bed on the verge of sleep, an upcoming scene often blossoms in my mind. I sometimes make notes on a piece of paper by my bed and transcribe them into the computer the next morning. At other times, I get up and type the new scene straight into the computer. If the scene isn't the next event in my story, I'll save it in a separate file I call bits.doc, knowing it's waiting on my hard drive for when I need it.

Before I had my first computer, I kept these notes on pieces of paper in a notebook, transcribing them when the time came. Because they were handwritten, I tended not to write them in much detail. I often lost the freshness of the scenes, forgetting details that were clear to me at the time of first imagining.

Reasons for Writing on Computer

- Corrections can be made without retyping entire pages.

- Paragraphs and pages can easily be moved from one location to another.

- Changes that affect the entire manuscript can be made in a moment. A character's name can be changed throughout the book using one "search and replace" command.

- Using a "find" command, you can locate a specific passage in seconds without shuffling through hundreds of manuscript pages.

- A complete copy of your manuscript can be made onto a disk in seconds, allowing you to keep a backup in your desk, your pocket, or your safety deposit box.

- With the spell check command on your word processor, you can find misspelled words you may have missed when proofreading.

- You can use the electronic thesaurus in your word processor to display synonyms of any highlighted word.

- If you have a laser printer, or a good quality bubble jet printer, you can produce a professional-looking, error-free manuscript for your publisher. If you don't, most towns and cities have a computer store that will print your manuscript from your disk onto a top-quality printer for a few dollars.

- Most publishers contracts specify that the writer will deliver both a paper copy of the manuscript and an electronic copy on disk.

c. Expanding your horizons

Although none of the following features are necessary for a romance writer, I've found they all save me work. I'd suggest you look into the ones that sound helpful to you, and ignore the rest. The templates and macros I have developed for my novels and book notes are available for most major word processors from Dogwood Technical Services Inc. (See the section on software, templates, and macros in Appendix 3.)

1. Templates save repetitive typing

In every book I write, the title page is identical except for the title and word count. The end of each chapter is followed by a page break. Each new chapter begins with the chapter name one third to half-way down the page.

After writing a few books, I realized the computer could do this repetitive work, and I created a template that contains all this repetitive typing, and styles to automate chapter headings and titles. For long books I use master and subdocument templates to break up the book into chapter files, yet read it as one file for printing, spell-checking, and revising.

I also use templates for my book notes. In my notes template, I have all the headings I usually use in book notes, as well as blank tables for my manuscript data sheet, character timelines, and chapter contents. (See Appendix 1.)

2. Macros help with revisions

Over the years I've developed a list of words and verb forms that often highlight weak writing. To save myself having to locate every instance of these words, when I'm beginning final revisions of my manuscript I run a macro that highlights questionable words in red. I then revise my manuscript, easily able to spot these words.

3. Software and the Internet help gather information

Writers need information. Depending where you live, a trip to the library may take hours, and you may not find the information you want there. More and more, it's possible to get information quickly while sitting at your computer. The following are examples of how I use software on my computer to get information. If you wish more information on the software and Internet resources mentioned below, see Appendix 3. For information on how to get on the Internet, check your local college or high school for night classes, or look up "Internet" in the yellow pages of your telephone book.

- I'm in my southern British Columbia home writing a scene that takes place February 14 in Mexico City. The heroine is meeting the hero at 7 p.m. for dinner. I need to know if it's light, dark, or twilight. I run *Almanac,* set my location to Mexico City and the date to February 14. I read the February 14 time for sunrise and sunset at Mexico City from my screen, then return to my writing.

- I'm choosing a name for a minor character. She's a female who I visualize as stiff and virtuous. I run the Dogwood Compendium of Names and search its 29,000 name database for female names meaning pure or virtuous. In a few seconds I have a list of names to choose from.

- My heroine is taking a trip from San Diego to Stockholm. I need to know how long the flight will be, when she'd leave San Diego, if she'll change planes, and what time she'll arrive in Stockholm. I click on the Internet icon on my computer and log onto an airline information Web page. I put in my heroine's travel requirements and within two minutes I have a screen displaying her flight information. I print the screen and disconnect from the Internet, then resume writing.

- I'm thinking of submitting my romance novel to a new publisher, but I want to know more about them first. I submit an e-mail message to RW-L, the Internet romance writers mailing list, asking if anyone has information about this publisher. A few hours later I get a response from a writer who just sold a book to this publisher.

d. Selecting a computer system

Before you start shopping for a computer, decide how much money you are willing to spend.

I know several professional writers who first began working on computer when a friend gave them an old relic that had been taking up space in the basement. At the other extreme, some writers spend thousands of dollars acquiring the latest state-of-the-art computer with high-speed laser printer and an expensive office software suite. As with most things, the more you are willing to spend, the more features you can buy.

Before you start shopping, decide how much money you're willing to spend. Then decide which of the features in the sections that follow are important to you and get as many of them as you can for your money.

1. What software will you be using?

Computer hardware is an empty shell into which you'll load programs to tell the computer how to do what you want. These programs are your software. As a writer, the most important program you'll load into your computer will be your word processor, the program that allows your computer to act as a complex typewriter with loads of extra features.

If you are completely unfamiliar with word processing and know a friend who uses a word processor, ask your friend for a demonstration. Otherwise, find a computer store with a helpful salesperson

Word Processor Features Useful for Writers

1. Ability to export files to standard formats.

2. Search and replace functions, allowing you to find all instances of a word or phrase, and replace it with another word or phrase (e.g., search for all references to "John" and replace with "Harold" when changing a character's name).

3. Ability to have two or more documents in memory at one time (e.g., your book notes and the current chapter you're working on).

4. Spelling checker. If the spelling checker dictionary isn't for the country your editor is located in, ask if alternate dictionaries are available from the software manufacturer.

5. Thesaurus. Try out the thesaurus and see if it's organized in a way that seems useful to you.

6. A grammar checker can be useful if you are weak in grammar, although it's no substitute for learning the rules of the English language.

7. Ability to change from normal view to outline view. This can be a great time saver for developing plot ideas.

8. Ability to define styles for standard paragraph formats, so that you change from normal style to chapter heading style and have all the formatting changes such as centering and capital letters applied automatically.

9. Ability to record macros. You can use macros to automate tasks such as searching for instances of weak words and highlighting them.

10. Ability to set up master and subdocuments to handle long books. The master document contains the formatting, title page, and a list of subdocument files. Each chapter can then be set up as a separate file which is automatically merged into the master document for printing, spellchecking, and other revising. Master document templates for Amipro, Microsoft Word for Windows, and WordPerfect are available from Dogwood Technical Services Inc. (see Appendix 3).

and ask for a demonstration. If you belong to a writers' group, ask other members what word processors they use.

If you're buying one of the major programs such as Microsoft Word, Corel WordPerfect, Lotus Word Pro, or Lotus Ami Pro, all the features you'll need as a writer will be included. If you're looking at a less expensive word-processing package, you'll want to check which features are offered.

When you use a word processor, your work will be saved in files. Although most word processors have their own unique file format, publishers usually have programs allowing them to accept a wide variety of formats and convert for use on their in-house system. If you're buying a word processor which is not one of those mentioned above, ask your computer salesperson if it has the ability to export files to standard file formats.

Once you know which program you're interested in, go to a computer store and look at the box containing your chosen word processor. Most manufacturers list the minimum hardware and operating system requirements to run the word processor. Write down this list and take it on your shopping trip.

2. What hardware do you need?

Once you've decided on your software, you'll need to go shopping for your software manufacturer's list of minimum hardware and operating system requirements. Go to at least two different computer stores. Give each one your list of minimum requirements and ask for a price quote. Also ask how long a warranty each store gives and how much help they're willing to give you if you have problems with the system. Depending on the amount of money you want to spend, you may decide to add some of the following features if they are not included in your list.

- **Modem** — If you're planning to connect to the Internet, you'll need a data modem. Call your Internet provider and ask what speed modem he or she recommends for connection. Most Internet providers will provide the software you need for Internet connection free of charge, with instructions on how to go about connecting. If you buy a fax/data modem, you'll also be able to send and receive faxes on your computer.

- **Monitor** — Be sure the display is clear and easy to look at; the smaller the dot pitch, the sharper the picture. A .28 dot pitch gives a sharper picture than a .39 dot pitch. An SVGA (super video graphic array) monitor is of higher quality than a VGA (video graphic array). A non-interlaced monitor is of higher quality than an interlaced one.

- **Printer** — A dot matrix printer is slower than a laser printer, produces poorer quality print, but is less expensive. You should know that many publishers will not accept manuscripts printed on dot matrix printers. Bubble jet printers vary in speed, and some are as fast as low-end laser printers. Bubble jet printers produce good quality print, some very close to laser quality, but if you plan to do a lot of printing you'll find the ink cartridges won't last long and will be expensive to replace. A

If you buy a fax/data modem, you'll be able to send and receive faxes on your computer.

laser printer usually costs more than either a dot matrix or bubble jet, but produces excellent quality print at good speed. The cost per copy for laser jet toner is lower than bubble jet ink.

- **Ergonomic furniture** — You need to think about your own "hardware" too — your hands, feet, and back. It's important you be able to type with minimum strain to your wrists and fingers. Many writers develop problems with carpal tunnel syndrome or tendinitis. Be sure your desk and chair allow you to type with shoulders and wrists relaxed. Consider an ergonomic keyboard that allows hands to rest at a natural angle. Be sure your chair gives sufficient support to your back. When your feet are flat on the floor, your knees should be level with or slightly higher than your hips. If not, get a foot rest or a better-fitting chair.

If you still have money in your budget at this point, your computer retailer will be glad to recommend options you might include in your system.

10.

Research

Your reader wants to pick up your novel and be transported into another world, to be held in the spell of your love story until the last page, then fall asleep with a sensation of lingering warmth. Your reader knows your story isn't real, but she's willing to pretend. Don't spoil it for her.

If your reader lives in British Columbia where you set your story, and you mention that your heroine drove from Vancouver to Victoria, she'll be jolted back to reality. Drove from Vancouver to Victoria? What a bunch of nonsense! This writer's never been to British Columbia.

Your hero and heroine buy a hamburger. Did they get it at McDonald's, MacDonald's, or MacDonalds? You think you're sure, but get out your phone book and check anyway.

Your heroine mails a manuscript from your home town to London, England. She puts ten dollars on the counter to pay air mail rate. How long is it since you mailed a manuscript to London? Contact the post office and check the rate.

Your hero is in the arctic in June. It's midnight. Is it actually light enough to read a newspaper the way you've heard? Get an almanac, or get on the Internet and check.

You've been to Mexico and you speak a little Spanish, so you've tossed a few Spanish words into your dialogue. Check a Spanish dictionary to be sure the spelling is correct. Check with the Spanish teacher at the local high school to see if your sentence is correctly phrased. If you can't find the answer, take the reference out of your book or give your character an excuse for the mistake, as I did in *After All This Time*:

Carrie murmured to Marisla, "Fugarse. Matrimonio fugarse." Momentarily Marisla looked confused, then newly excited.

Jane was laughing. "You told her you ran away to get married?"

"I think I got the grammar wrong."

a. Researching settings

From 1987 to 1989 I lived in Mexico. I became very familiar with the country, the people, and their social customs as experienced by an English-speaking foreigner. I set several books in Mexico, but despite the fact I'd lived in Mexico I also did a great deal of research on the country.

In my research, I focused on books written for people who will be spending some time in Mexico, not tourist books for quick trips to the tourist centers. In particular, I used a book called *The People's Guide to Mexico,* written for people taking extended trips to Mexico. It's filled with a wealth of information, including the meaning of hand signals used by Mexicans, religious holidays and festivals, and differences in customs in different areas of the country. This book gave me a feel for Mexico beyond my own experience. I also used other books when I needed to check information I couldn't find in *The People's Guide.*

To get a feel for a location or country, look for biographical travel accounts where the writer actually lived among the local people, and cruising and camping guides that give the writers' personal experiences. Talk to people who have been there recently. Ask what they remember best, what they liked best, and what they disliked. Ask if they'd mind reading parts of your story when you're done to check for location accuracy.

As your plot develops, keep a list of the things you need to check. The heroine is traveling in Mexico. She has to go to the dentist. Is the dentist likely to speak English? If not, how will the meeting go? If you can't figure it out and you don't know anyone who's been to a dentist in a Latin American country, try asking on a newsgroup on the Internet. The answers you get may cause you to change your plans for the scene, but the result will be better.

If you're not expert on your setting, it's wise to have your viewpoint character new to the setting as well. Any mistakes the character makes will then seem natural.

If you're not an expert on your setting, it's wise to have your character new to the setting as well.

1. When Love Returns

My hero in *With Strings Attached* was one of two brothers who had grown up on a farm. My experience of farms was limited, but because the farm was only background color and my hero wasn't living there, my own experience of living in a rural community was sufficient research for the setting.

As I wrote the book, I became intrigued by my hero's older brother who ran the family farm. By the time I finished *Strings*, I knew I had to give David his own happy ending, which I did in my book *When Love Returns*.

Because part of David's love story would be set on the farm, I needed a realistic feel for that setting, and I needed to be sure I didn't get my facts wrong. I have a friend who owns a ranch, so I decided this farm would be a ranch like my friend's — a seed stock farm breeding Limousin cattle. I asked my friend to help me with research.

To be safe, I wrote most scenes involving the farm from the heroine's viewpoint, and made it clear she knew nothing about farming. I let her ask questions, and I posed those same questions to my friend to find out what David's answers would be. Then, after I'd written the scenes involving farm matters, I called my friend and read passages to her, to be sure David's farm talk was consistent with the way a seed stock cattle rancher would talk.

David and Julie made love for the first time in the hayloft of the barn. At one point in the scene I needed to know the name of the door that opens at the top of the barn to load and unload hay. I called my ranching friend, but she didn't know of any special name for the door. I called another friend who'd been brought up on a farm and got the same answer. Still, I knew there might be a proper name for that door. Since the door featured in the scene, I had Julie ask David what it was called, then later — after they'd made love — I had her realize that he'd never answered her question.

2. *How to write about a place you've never been*

When my editor requested I write a book set in South America, I began playing with the idea. How could I write a believable romance novel set in South America when I'd never been there? First, I decided, I should pick a country where they speak Spanish. I'd lived in Mexico, so I'd have the advantage of familiarity with the language.

I needed to know if the people of the country I picked were at all like the Latin American people I'd met in Mexico. Would the men behave with the same courtesy toward women? Would the women wear high heels, tight skirts, and faultless make-up?

I found a book on Latin American customs for travelers. This wonderful reference book was divided into countries, giving accepted greetings and customs for each country. From it I learned that in Peru when an unmarried woman is kissed three times on the cheek as a greeting, the first two kisses are the greeting. The third is a wish for the woman's marriage.

Three kisses and a wish for a marriage. Ideas began stirring in my subconscious.

Peru has many historical sites of the Inca who once ruled so much of South America. In college, I'd taken archaeology and been fascinated by the Inca. I went to the library and brought home armloads of books about Peru and the Inca. I decided my heroine would be an American who had come to Peru summer after summer with her archaeologist father, studying the ruins.

When I needed to know how much of this history was reflected in modern Peru, I found the answer in *Cut Stones and Crossroads* by Ronald Wright, an account of an archaeologist's travels through the Peru he loves so much. From this book I got a feel for the remote mountain villages of Peru, where people still live history, and a reassurance that the Peruvians of Spanish descent were much like their Mexican counterparts in manner and behavior.

I decided to make my hero of Spanish descent, educated in England and the United States. I knew from my research that many wealthy Peruvian families send their children away to northern countries for their education, and I felt more comfortable with a hero who was somewhat Anglicized.

My conflict would be rooted in the mixed cultural background of my hero and heroine. My heroine would be a modern North American woman with a career she valued. Although he loved her, my hero would be a Peruvian whose wife must take her place in the family hacienda, whose children would be brought up to their ancient heritage.

Because of the research involved, *Catalina's Lover* was harder work than most of my other romance novels, but I enjoyed writing it tremendously and when my agent read it and told me he felt as if he'd been there, I knew I'd done a good job on the research.

b. Researching historical novels

If your characters act out their romantic story in another time, you'll need to research not only the location, but also the historical period. You're unlikely to get all the information you need from a live interview. You'll need to read books about the period. In doing this research, focus on what life felt like in the time you're writing about. People of every age are primarily concerned with survival and relationships. Research to find the differences. What sort of careers could a woman have? How easy was it for a man to pack up his belongings and move to another town? As with any research, always check the details. Did zippers exist in your story period? Running water? Electric lights?

Kathi Webb on...Researching to Write Historical Romance

In this high-tech age I still like to research the old-fashioned way: through books. I read everything I can about the time period I'm writing in, particularly journals and first-person accounts. Whenever possible, I visit recreated old sites of townships or houses containing original furnishings and household items of yesteryear. Some of my most helpful research books have been purchased in children's bookstores. The illustrations and details depicted are simple, yet provide enough information to be blended effortlessly into my stories. Recently I found a wonderful book of paper doll clothes, a journal of fashion history.

It's important not to get so carried away by the period details that you lose sight of a writer's main task, that of telling a compelling story with interesting characters while making the setting a minor character. I believe this applies whether one writes historical, contemporary, or futuristic romances.

One thing I try to avoid is old western movies. I love them, but find they provide a very "Hollywood" interpretation of life a hundred or more years ago. Since I want my work to evolve from the essence of who I am and how I feel things, I write by instinct, from knowing my characters so intimately that it's an easy matter to transfer their words, thoughts, and feelings from my head to the reader's page.

c. Researching occupations and lifestyles

When I meet someone who works in an occupation that interests me, I'll often ask if I can interview that person regarding his or her work. Sometimes I'll have a story in mind. When I don't, by the time I'm done the interview I've usually got a new story growing.

In 1989 Brian and I sailed north from Cabo San Lucas to San Diego in the company of another sailboat crewed by friends. We'd known Jill and Nigel for two years and I'd always been fascinated by Nigel's summertime career as captain of an icebreaker in the Beaufort Sea.

I interviewed him one evening in a remote anchorage on the west coast of the Baja, using my small tape recorder to take down the conversation. Interviewing Nigel, I knew that if I could portray a few authentic moments in a sea captain's day, my readers would feel they'd been on board with him.

When I asked how he got to his ship, Nigel described flying from Calgary to Tuktoyaktuk in northern Canada where he changed into anti-exposure coveralls against the cold before he got into the helicopter that would fly to his ship. I asked the function of his ship, and he told me it was to tend to the oil rig, which was also a large ship.

I knew that Nigel called home by radio once a week. I asked him where he called from. From the oil rig, he said, explaining how he got from the icebreaker to the oil rig in a man basket. My imagination was caught by the image of a man getting into a wire cage and letting himself be hauled into the air by a crane, swung over the deck of the oil rig, and set down — all to spend five minutes on the phone with the woman he loved. I was determined to put the man basket into my book.

I asked, "What's it like being out in a storm? What's scary about it? What's dangerous?"

Soon I was listening to an account of an ice pack drifting down on the oil rig, the icebreaker crew hauling seven-ton Bruce anchors on deck. A dangerous activity, and one I knew would make a tense moment in my book.

By the time I finished interviewing Nigel, I had two hours of tape to transcribe and several sketches of man baskets and Bruce anchors. I also had a story idea. Some months later I finished *The Touch of Love*, a novel in which my hero was captain of an icebreaker in the Beaufort Sea. I dedicated the book to Jill and Nigel.

d. Researching motivations and issues

You've decided that your hero owns a winery in California. You are looking for conflict as you develop your characters. You decide your heroine grew up in an alcoholic family and is frightened by any contact with alcohol. If you yourself grew up in an alcoholic family, chances are you know exactly how this woman will feel and behave as she falls in love with the hero. You can imagine yourself falling in love with such a man, and explore your own feelings and reactions to the fantasy. You'll journey inward to your own memories and reactions, to explore your heroine's motivation and backstory.

But what if you grew up in a healthy family where alcohol was something your parents consumed only at Christmas and Easter?

Fortunately, the answers to your research questions about almost any childhood trauma are as near as the self-help section of your local bookstore. Look for books written to help survivors of trauma and dysfunction. These books often begin with a list of characteristics common to survivors. You'll quickly learn that the heroine of your alcoholic family probably has control issues that make her react whenever anyone makes her feel trapped, and the urge to run when she thinks an argument might erupt. She may be very successful, driven to perfectionism, but have an underlying conviction that she can never be good enough. Her choice of profession was probably influenced by her sibling-order position in the alcoholic family.

Whether your hero was a battered child or became a grieving widower two years ago, there's a book on the shelves that describes what he's feeling now.

Whether your hero was a battered child or became a grieving widower two years ago, there's a book on the shelves that describes what your character is feeling, how he's likely to be acting, and what's needed for his recovery. Since your heroine is going to help him recover, you need to know what's required.

Whether your heroine was raped two years ago and can't handle physical intimacy, or grew up with a physical disability that has her in a wheelchair, there's a book on the shelves describing how she feels about her injuries and herself. Read it, and write a realistic heroine who overcomes her problems with passion and realism and the emotional support of a man who loves her.

e. Research sources

1. People

It's always worthwhile to interview someone who has first-hand knowledge of what you plan to write about. Approach your subject and explain that you're a writer researching a novel. You're interested in his job, her recent experiences in Greece, his knowledge about what it's like to have both legs broken and walk on crutches for four months. If the subject seems willing, set a future time for the interview. This will give you both time to prepare.

Be sure your subject understands you are not planning to write the book about him or her as a person. You might want to explain that you don't write about real people, although real experiences and events sometimes give the spark for fictional ideas.

Plan a list of questions in advance, but go to the interview ready to abandon your plan and take a new direction. Follow up on any intriguing comments that interest you. When I interviewed Nigel, I hadn't planned an accident at sea for my book until he explained the dangerous process of raising anchors in a storm.

Bring paper for notes and at least two pens to write with. If you have a small tape recorder, bring it and ask the person if you can tape the conversation. Most people are willing to be taped, especially if you explain you're not planning to put their words into a book, but simply to have an accurate record of what they said.

Some professionals — doctors, police officers, prosecutors — may be hesitant to answer speculative "what if" questions. Reassure your subject that you write fiction. You only want to know how a person in this job might react if the event you've described happens.

As you ask questions, look for the feel of the job, the setting, or the experience.

Thank your subject when you're finished, and ask if he or she would be willing to answer more questions that come up as you're writing the book. If you plan to acknowledge your subject's contribution, be sure you check the spelling of the name.

As soon as you can, sit down at your computer and transcribe the interview tape. Some words and phrases will be difficult to make out. It will be easier if you do the transcription while the conversation is fresh in your mind. If you didn't make a tape, sit down at your

Transcribe your tape while the interview is fresh in your mind; it will be easier than trying to do it after considerable time has passed.

computer immediately after the conversation and write a detailed account from your notes. I've always been amazed at how much detail I can remember when I do this.

Remember that you're writing fiction. The material you've learned from your subject may form the basis for a character or event, but feel free to have your character react differently, or to have fate treat your character differently.

2. Books and magazines

One of the most useful magazines I've ever subscribed to is the *Financial Post*. Every month this magazine has an excellent profile of a manager in a different industry. One month featured a corporate private investigator. Another featured a woman who was chief executive officer of a mining company. Yet another profiled executives in the phone-sex trade. I clip these articles and file them along with similar articles from other magazines. They're wonderful sparks for growing characters.

I'm always on the lookout for useful books — not only books to help me write the current novel, but ones that might be useful in the future. For years, whenever I saw a book on gypsies in a secondhand store, I'd buy it and add it to my collection. When I wrote *The Dance of Seduction*, my gypsy research formed the basis for my heroine.

Like many writers, I collect information. Scraps about gypsies, about mining executives, about television news people. These scraps provide compost, fertilizer for new stories, whether they're in my library or only in my mind. Cultivate the habit of curiosity, of picking up books on subjects that interest you. A book can be every bit as valuable as a knowledgeable, cooperative interview subject.

> **Cultivate the habit of curiosity.**

f. The Internet

When I can't find the fact I need in my own bookshelves, I usually turn to the Internet. If you're not familiar with the Internet, I'd recommend you read one of the many books available on the topic. For a list of Internet sites for romance writers, see Appendix 3.

1. World Wide Web

The World Wide Web is a massive network of information pages accessible through the Internet. Think of each Web page as the cover of a magazine, in a massive store filled with magazines. Using a browser such as Netscape or Microsoft's Internet Explorer, you can perform a search of the World Wide Web. Most browsers have a button you can click on with your mouse to go to a search function. Searching for "arson" or "Greece" will usually result in a massive list of links to other Web pages. Think of this list as a table of contents in a magazine. Click on one and you'll move to the information it references, much as you would turn to an article in a magazine.

2. Libraries

Among the wealth of information on the Internet is access to many public and university libraries and periodical indexes. If you're looking for the exact title of a book by Stephen King, the year *Wuthering Heights* was written, or the ISBN (international standard book number) of the new novel you want your bookstore to order, try the Internet.

3. Newsgroups

The Internet hosts thousands of newsgroups. These newsgroups are divided into interest areas, each providing a storage area for messages from around the world about a specific topic. Most of these newsgroups are open to anyone who wants to visit. Think of each one as a massive filing cabinet of messages about a certain topic. The topic is defined in a newsgroup's title: alt.romance, alt.authorware, alt.astrology, and alt.law-enforcement are only a few of thousands of newsgroups on the Internet. When you use your Web browser to perform a search, the list of results will sometimes include newsgroup articles. If you want to visit a specific newsgroup, most browsers include a newsreader to scroll through newsgroups.

If your search for information fails to produce the data you need, locate a newsgroup relating to your topic and post a message asking for information. If you don't want to revisit the newsgroup to check for your answers, ask to have answers sent directly to your e-mail address.

4. Mailing lists

In addition to the wealth of open newsgroups on the Internet, there are numerous subscribed mailing lists which send out messages posted by members. Romance writers will want to subscribe to RW-L, the romance writers' list, which is open to anyone interested in writing romance. RW-L is a free service subscribed to by many unpublished and published writers on the Internet. See section **d.** in Appendix 3 for instructions on subscribing.

Locate a newsgroup relating to your topic, and post a message asking for information.

If you're looking for someone who has experience at being a police officer or driving a truck, or who suffers from carpal tunnel syndrome, or has visited Spain, try your writer's list. Chances are one of the writers has the information you need.

No matter how supportive your friends and family are, they're unlikely to understand your passion for non-existent people and events the way another writer can. You may have access to local writers' groups, or you may live in an isolated location where the nearest group is a hundred miles away. If you're connected to the Internet, you'll be able to commune with other writers no matter where you live.

5. Growing with the Internet

The Internet is changing daily. To explore its ever-growing possibilities, pick up one of many current books on the subject. Internet books range from "easy-to-read" to "technobabble." Before you buy one, see if you find the writing easy to understand.

There are many courses available about the Internet. Before signing up, ask what the instructor will be covering and whether you'll get time on the Internet as part of the course. Most introductory courses cover the basics of how to send and receive e-mail, how to begin browsing the World Wide Web, and how to search and post to newsgroups.

11.

Priorities, goals, and the garbage can

a. Priorities and goals

1. The single most important thing

To sell a romance novel, you must first finish the book.

One of the most effective ways to motivate yourself to keep writing is to set goals: goals about how many pages you'll write each day or week or goals about when you plan to finish your first draft. If you write two pages every day, you'll have your book done in less than six months.

What your writing goals are will depend on the circumstances of your life and how much time you plan to give to your writing. I think of my writing goals as objectives and, like my vision of my story's plot, I modify and revise my goals as I go along with the book.

Here are some writing goals you might decide to adopt:

- Write at least two pages a day until the book is finished.
- Write at least five days a week.
- Finish the first draft of the book before Christmas.
- Finish chapter 1 by the end of the month.

2. A place to write

When my children were small and I was an unpublished novelist, I wrote in the living room while the kids napped, stopping when I heard the cry of the first one wakening. Later, they stopped napping and I began writing evenings. As they became teenagers and stayed up later than I did, I realized I needed a place of my own to write.

You'll find it much easier to achieve your writing goals if you have a time and place to write where you're uninterrupted. If you're writing on the dining room table, it could be difficult to find writing time. If getting ready to write means clearing the dishes and chasing the kids into their bedrooms to do homework, it may be impossible to claim your writing time.

Find a corner that's your own and fill it with your computer and the reference books you use most often. If the place you've chosen isn't working, find somewhere else.

When I realized the open office in my house wasn't working because of too many interruptions, I asked Brian to gut our small travel trailer of bunks and tables and build in a desk and stereo for me. We put everything I need to write into that old trailer, including a warm carpet and a coffee pot. I named it "my studio" and it's the best writing place I've ever had. Probably the best thing about it is that there's no telephone to tempt me with interruptions.

Take a look at your home. Find the best solution you can, the best place to write with minimum interruptions, whether it's the bedroom or the garage. Tell your family what you need and ask for their help to create a writing place for you.

3. Writing in circles

When I began selling novels, I naturally wanted to write the best prose I could. I would write chapter 1. Then I'd reread it and revise it until I felt happy with it. That done, I'd go on with chapter 2. At the end of chapter 2, I'd be aware of improvements I could make to chapter 1 in light of the events in chapter 2. I'd revise chapters 1 and 2, then write chapter 3. I would continue the book in this pattern, so that by the end of the first draft I would have revised chapter 1 eleven times, and chapter 12 not at all. Interestingly enough, I usually found that the final chapters of the book needed less revision. By the time I wrote them, I knew my characters intimately, I was clear on exactly what needed to happen to achieve the story goal, and my writing seemed to emerge free of awkwardness. In doing my final revisions, I would sometimes realize than much of the first two chapters was not actually necessary to the book. My much-revised chapter 1 was often consigned to the garbage and never appeared in the printed book.

Despite the fact that this pattern was producing salable books, I was aware of a constant yearning to simply *write* the story instead of continually going back and revising. I began to wonder what would happen if I wrote the first draft without stopping to revise.

I decided to experiment on my seventh book, writing steadily without going back, pushing down the panicky feeling that I was going too fast. Amazingly, the book was finished in a fraction of the time the others took, I had fewer revisions to do than on previous books, and for the first time my editor didn't ask for any changes.

Since then I've become flexible about whether I revise as I go. I usually begin a day's writing by looking over what I wrote the day before. Reading through the passage on the computer screen gets me into the flow of the story, and I often make minor revisions as I'm reading. On the other hand, I don't go back to revise beyond the previous day's work unless I have a specific reason, such as changing an important historical detail for one of my characters. When I become aware of minor changes that need to be made for consistency, I write them down on a Post-it note and stick it to my computer monitor. When I finish the first draft, I attend to all the notes I've made as I went along.

As you write your novel, you'll become aware of passages you've written that need improvement. You may feel the urge to go back and make the passage perfect before you go on to the next chapter. You may become aware your heroine didn't react in the way she really would react when you wrote the last chapter. You may need to go back and rewrite the scene before you go on, because her changed behavior could affect the course of the rest of the book.

A certain amount of fiddling with what you've written is healthy for the book, but if you try to make each chapter perfect as you go along, you may never finish. Tell yourself you can polish later, but right now you must get on with the story. Finish your first draft, get the story to its end. Don't let yourself get stuck in one place without forward movement.

b. Writer's block and the garbage can

When I first became a published novelist, I understood writer's block to mean that a writer wants to write, but somehow can't get words down on paper. I decided writer's block was a psychosomatic illness. If I believed in it, it would happen to me. If I didn't, it wouldn't.

1. Doubt and confusion

Although I still believe writer's block is something that happens if you expect it to, I also know that sometimes the words stop for no reason I can determine, and a perfectly good story idea curls into an uncooperative ball of meaningless details. When this happens, I'll find myself examining the book, asking: "What's this story really about? Who are these people? What am I about as a writer?"

I've written over two dozen women's fiction novels and two thrillers in the last 12 years. In that time, doubt and confusion have attacked me many times. Every writer I've asked has also admitted to having attacks of self-doubt and confusion, unwanted halts in the progress of a book. Whether we call it writer's block or not, it happens.

What can we do to get things going again? Should we fight with our characters? Sit down and write regardless? Cry? Throw the book away and try another story? Over the years, I've tried every one of these tactics, trying to understand what the easy flow of words is about, and why the words sometimes stop.

2. The ebb and flow of writing

In writing a novel, I've found there's a natural pattern, an ebb and flow that repeats itself book after book. From discussions with other writers, I've learned each writer has his or her own natural pattern. It's different for each, and it can change during a writer's career.

> Each writer has his or her own natural writing pattern.

In recognizing this natural flow, I've learned that sometimes when my words stop it's a normal part of my writing process. I can relax, knowing that soon the words will start again. Because I try not to fight them, these natural pauses tend to be briefer than they once were.

Here's my usual pattern in writing a novel: I get an idea, usually a scene or part of a scene I find exciting. I can feel the energy behind this idea, though I don't usually have a clear picture of the story. I'll write a few pages, perhaps half a chapter. Then I'll stop, realizing I don't know who these people are, where they came from, or where they're going. My subconscious tossed the spark to me. I know there's a story here, but if I try to write it now, I'll grind to a halt.

I need to wait for my creative mind to serve up the whole picture. If I'm not working on another book when the new idea comes, I focus on clearing the decks, getting ready to write. I pay my bills, clean my desk, enjoy a brief holiday from my computer and remind myself that when I go back, I'll know what the new story is about. If I get ideas, I make a note of them, then go on clearing my decks. Usually, by the time my desk and my house are clean, I'm ready to start writing character backgrounds.

Sometimes a story spark lies in my mind for a long time before the pieces fall into place.

When I do begin writing the book, the first three chapters are always the hardest. With every scene I'm introducing a new character or a new environment to the reader. I have to orient the reader, give enough background to avoid confusion, yet keep the pace moving fast so description and narrative don't kill the reader's interest. I'm often aware of fears that there really isn't a story here, that the people won't come to life on my computer screen. I ask myself what this story is about, whether I have a story at all, whether the reader will give a damn.

As much as I can, I push these doubts aside and move on to write the next scene, telling myself I can always revise it later.

Usually I find that by pushing on past this difficult part of writing a book, putting my rear end in the chair and forcing myself to write, I move on to the essence of the book. Many of those early doubts are only my own insecurities, my natural fears of starting a new project.

3. Getting started

Getting started is always the hardest part of writing. Writing the first chapter, the first sentence, the first word. To prevent myself from facing this problem, if I finish a scene during the day's writing, I'll usually go on and begin the next scene, get it started so I'm not looking at a blank page when I sit at my computer the next day. I begin my day's writing by rereading what I wrote the day before, revising it on the screen as I reread. Usually by the time I get to the end of yesterday's work, my mind is focused on the book and I simply carry on writing.

> **Getting started is the hardest part of writing.**

If I come to the end of yesterday's work and stop dead, I usually force myself to write at least one paragraph, but if it's not working after that, I'll let myself stop for the day. When I come back the next day, if the words won't flow, I'll backtrack to the previous scene. Often, I'll find I've taken a wrong turn somewhere in that scene. Once I've fixed it, the words begin flowing again.

4. Listening to yourself

A couple of years ago, a writer working on a non-fiction project asked me for advice on her writer's block. She'd realized half-way through her book that she had to expand the scope of her work, that every topic in her book had a new level of meaning she hadn't explored. "I'm stuck," she said. "I know what I want to write, but I can't seem to make myself work on the book. I procrastinate and feel guilty, but I haven't worked on it in a year. I wish I could just go ahead, write the new chapters, but first I have to go back and revise all those early chapters, include the new material, and I can't seem to make myself do it."

When I asked why she couldn't write the new chapters first, her face brightened as if I'd taken a load from her. She wanted to work on the new chapters, her energy was there, but she hadn't been able to give herself permission because she thought she must revise the older chapters first.

Listen to your impulses about writing. Listen to your impulses about writing. If you want to write the last chapter of your novel first, why not try it and see if it works? Agatha Christie often wrote the final scene of her books first. It might work for you, or it might not. Why not experiment?

When I'm having trouble getting back to writing, I examine the little thoughts that come to me. If I hear myself say, "I wish I could jump over this part and get on to the interesting stuff," I'll leap over the part I don't want to write, tell myself I'll write it later, but right now I want to get back to writing something. When I do this, I usually find the part I didn't want to write doesn't belong in the book at all. The reader can leap over the missing section of time as easily as I can (see chapter 19).

If a leap over time won't work, I try changing points of view. I was going to write the next scene from the heroine's point of view. What if I write it from the hero's? Does that make it easier to get going?

If I try all these things, but the story still won't write itself, I try the garbage can test.

5. The garbage can test

I developed the garbage can test on impulse several years ago while giving a weekend workshop to a group of writers. One of the writers had a complicated plot. I knew the story had a problem. There were bad guys and a sheriff and a heroine's brother in prison. I couldn't make sense of the characters' motivations. I was confused because I didn't know what part of this chaos was important to the writer. I didn't know what to suggest she keep, or what to urge her to throw away. I didn't know where to focus my attempts to fix the story.

On impulse, I held up her manuscript. "Okay," I said. "We both know there's a problem and we don't know how to fix it. Let's pretend for a minute that I'm going to throw this manuscript into the garbage."

She leaned forward in her seat, hands gripping the arms of her chair. I dropped the manuscript onto the floor beside me.

"It's gone. Into the garbage. You're never going to be able to write it now. You'll never see the characters again. I want you to think about that."

I could feel her thinking.

"If you could reach in and pick out just one part of that story, just one thing you don't want to let go of, what would it be?"

What she picked surprised me, because I hadn't known what was important to her in the story. It wasn't the sheriff or the brother in jail. It wasn't the bad guys. It was something I'd lost sight of. It was the restaurant where all this confusing action was set, the restaurant which had become lost in a herd of characters with complicated problems. I don't know whether she went on to write the story, but I have to thank that writer for giving me the motivation to come up with the garbage can test.

A few weeks later, I told Naomi Horton about the garbage can. Naomi was stalled in her book at the time. When she tried the garbage can, she realized the thing she cared about was the hero she'd visualized, a man who had lived undercover so long he was more accustomed to lies than truth. She realized she was writing the book with the wrong heroine. She threw out her planned heroine and wrote *No Lies Between Us* with a heroine whose motivation and backstory fit the hero — a woman who vowed she'd never be lied to again.

The next time I attended one of Naomi's lectures, I heard her mention the Vanessa Grant Garbage Can Test. I put the test in my own arsenal of writer's tools, and later used it myself in writing *Yesterday's Vows*.

Since writing *Yesterday's Vows*, I've used the garbage can test at some point on almost every book I've written. In the rare event when it hasn't worked, it's been because I've been at a point in my life as a writer where I need to take a break, where I have to step back from writing and re-examine my goals and myself as a person. Perhaps I've received a rejection from a publisher I expected to want my work. Rejections don't necessarily mean there's anything wrong

Using the Garbage Can

Has your idea ground to a halt? Are your characters going down in quicksand? Do you wonder what the point of your story is? Try using the garbage can…

- Sit in a comfortable chair, take a few deep breaths and relax.

- Close your eyes and imagine you are holding your story in your hands — your notes, whatever pages of manuscript you've written, every scrap of paper relating to this story.

- Visualize yourself throwing the story and all its papers into your garbage can. If you have trouble imagining this, collect the papers together and physically throw them into an empty garbage can.

- Tell yourself it's gone. You'll never be able to write that story now.

- If you could reach in and pick out just one part of that story, one thing you don't want to let go of, what would it be?

- Let everything else in the story go. Begin a new story, starting from that one thing.

with a writer's work, yet every writer I know feels a sense of personal failure when a rejection arrives.

To fight the effects of rejection, I know I must immediately affirm my own worth as a person and as a writer. I've learned to seek out my husband, tell him I'm depressed, and listen when he says he believes in me. If I need more, I phone an affirming writer friend. And I take out my "warm fuzzy album."

6. Creating a warm fuzzy album

A couple of years ago, I attended a networking lecture by a woman named Pat Nichol. In the course of the lecture, she mentioned that she kept a warm fuzzy album of affirming messages, compliments from people who'd attended her lectures, and loving cards from her children.

That night, I started my own warm fuzzy album. In it I put ammunition to fight the feeling of low self-worth that attacks us all at times. When someone says something complimentary about me or my writing, I often ask them to write the thought in a card and give it to me so I can put it in my warm fuzzy album. I also have cards from my children there, reminding me I'm a good mother, a good person. I have valentines from my husband, to remind me I'm loved, and letters from people who attended my lectures and said I helped them.

When I'm feeling low, I take out my warm fuzzy album and look through it. By the time I reach the end, I've taken the first step back to self-confidence, to finding myself again as a writer and a person.

7. Protecting the embryo

Most writers I know rarely talk about the parts of a book they haven't written yet. They've learned to fear that their growing ideas will be distorted or even destroyed by outside input. Some writers don't talk about their books at all until they are finished writing them.

When you do talk about your work, or show your work, be careful. Think of your formative story as an embryo, an unborn child. Protect it. Explain exactly what you want to the person you're sharing with. If you need to know whether your plot works, but don't want style or grammar criticized, say so. If the critic tells you what's wrong with your grammar anyway, stop the words by saying, "Right now I want to know only about the plot."

If a critic leaves you feeling inadequate about yourself as a writer and discouraged about your book, avoid sharing your work with that person again. On the other hand, if you come away from contact with someone you've shown your work to with a head full of new ideas, or if a critic points out a flaw and you think, "I know how to fix that. I knew something was wrong and now I understand," then you've received valuable help. Read *The Artist's Way* by Julia Cameron for wonderful advice about making sure you accept only useful criticism, and guidelines on how to recognize destructive criticism. Read *Bird by Bird* by Anne Lamott for advice on surviving discouragement in a writer's life.

Part 3

From spark to finish —
how a story grows

12.

Where do you get your ideas?

Some years ago, I'd had the beginning of a story idea that excited me, and I needed to share it with another writer. I phoned Naomi Horton and shared the idea with her.

A woman looks over the crowd in a Mexican marketplace and recognizes a man on the far side of the crowd. The instant she recognizes him, she runs in panic.

Being a real storyteller, Naomi got excited about my idea and we began brainstorming.

Why did the woman run? Who was the man? I suggested she'd run because of some shameful secret, that the hero had been watching news on TV and saw her. Perhaps the heroine had been declared dead and there was a big inheritance about to be distributed, and the hero would gain from this. But the instant he saw her on the news he took off after her, to bring her back because he wanted her alive.

Why should she run on sight of him? Naomi suggested it might have something to do with guns and criminals. No, I said, not this story. I'm writing this story.

Two years after this phone call, Naomi and I used my Mexican market idea to develop a day-long workshop in which we showed how each of us would take this story spark and develop it into a book. I believe the reason this workshop has been so popular is that it illustrates the ways in which every storyteller is unique, and also what we have in common.

Each writer must find the way of working that works for her or him. As you read how I developed this story idea, take what's of use to you and file away the rest.

a. From spark to idea

I was hooked on the image of a woman spotting a man across a crowded market, then running. I'd written a couple of pages that might make the first scene and I liked the feel of them. She dashes out of the market, terrified he might have seen her, looking back as she runs. She flees to a small vegetable market a few blocks away and gets her breath, panic pounding. He hasn't followed her. She's alone, safe. But if he saw her, she isn't safe. Her safety depends on him having no idea where to look for her.

Now my heroine must stop panicking and start thinking, but before I can write her thoughts, I need answers myself.

Who is she? Why did she run? Does she know the man? Who is he? Is he the hero? Did she leave him? If so, why? A shameful secret? A disputed inheritance? Is she missing? Declared dead? If missing, how did he find her? Accident? TV news? Why is she in Mexico?

b. Development and standstill

I needed to figure out who these people were. I needed to know what motivated them, what their dreams and fears were. I also needed to know that when I put hero and heroine together, their goals and hang-ups would drive them into conflict.

I decided the heroine's name was Jan, and she was in La Paz, Mexico.

1. Why is Jan in a Mexican market?

I remembered a woman I met in Mexico, a Canadian who made her living exporting Mexican crafts to Canada. She lived a very basic existence, staying on other people's boats, sleeping on other people's sofas, but she was legally a resident of Mexico and had been for about five years. She was making a sparse living.

If this is Jan's situation, why is she in Mexico? If she's been married to this man, and has left, what reason explains her need to disappear so completely that she leaves her own country? The obvious reason would be that he is abusive, that she is physically afraid of him, but I wanted this man to be the hero, not the villain.

Perhaps she married him for love and discovered on her wedding day that he married her for a merger, to join her family's assets to his. What sort of assets? A ranch?

2. Who is the hero?

Who is this hero? Is he rich? Powerful? Perhaps she's rich. They married and her disappearance leaves him in control of her money. It's been seven years since she left and she's about to be declared dead. (Is it true that people can be declared dead after seven years? They seem to do it quicker on television. Must find out.) The other relatives want her declared dead because they want the estate wound up. He's haunted, still loves her. Then he sees her on a news shot on television, doesn't even know if it's her, but he must find out.

I'm getting a feeling for him, but if she doesn't have a good reason for leaving, the whole thing falls apart. Why not just get a divorce?

3. What's their problem?

Maybe they lived on the Canadian Gulf Islands. Maybe their parents co-owned a piece of property. When it was split up, *her* father got the water rights to *his* father's land. Then her dad got nasty and cut off water access. To right the wrong, she marries the hero. But why go to Mexico? Why not simply go to the city and work there, even if she can't divorce him because...

The story was getting complicated. I kept adding details, explaining things to myself. I decided I had to kill someone to get her to come home for the funeral. The Mexican market was lost somewhere, but I had a lot of detailed notes.

Then another writer said something about these land problems sounding complicated, and she asked me a question. Not only couldn't I answer, I didn't even want to. I had Mexican markets, water rights, and Canadian ranches. I had a presumed-dead heroine, a marriage, a formless hero who nonetheless was determined to get the heroine. It was a mess: a complicated setup with complex motivations I didn't believe in. It wasn't a story, just a heap of ideas.

My story had become a complicated setup with complex motivations I didn't believe in.

4. The garbage can test

I threw the Mexican market into my garbage can, told myself it was gone, done. Then I asked myself what I didn't want to let go of. And there was one thing: A woman looks across a crowd and sees a man, then runs in panic when she recognizes him.

It didn't matter if it was a Mexican market, that was only local color. What mattered was her feeling of panic when she saw him. I felt she hadn't seen this man in a long time, they'd been married and she had left him. That's certainly not a story, but I'd succeeded in stripping away a bunch of nonessentials such as the Mexican market and the arranged marriage.

Now I waited for the universe to toss me another idea — something I could add to the spark and get fertilization and a story.

I had a sense of what I was missing now.

I needed the right hero for this idea to work.

c. *Finding the hero*

Then I read an article about a television journalist who wrote a book about the television industry, and something clicked. I remembered that in the Gulf War a CNN journalist disappeared and everyone feared he was dead. He turned up a few days later with the inside story, amid talk of how he'd disappeared twice before, presumed dead in the midst of world turmoil. Both times he turned up with the inside story.

I began fantasizing another television journalist hooked on getting his story. This was the man my heroine had run from. The man who can get any story, who is always there in the hot spots, who cares passionately about truth. A fascinating man, but if you married him you'd see more of him on television than across the kitchen table.

I knew that with this hero and my runaway heroine, the story would come.

d. *From idea to plot*

1. *Growing characters*

Up until this point, the market story had been more work than fun, but with the introduction of the hero excitement began for me. I decided the hero's name was Connar. But for my heroine, I needed a name that described someone more uncontrollable, more passionate than a "Jan." I settled on Dixie.

Dixie ran away from her marriage to Connar because she felt too vulnerable. Perhaps he'd betrayed her in some way, and she couldn't stay to face it out. She was obviously impulsive, having run away. Impulsive and vulnerable — those were her weaknesses. I wanted her to have strengths as well, ones that would appeal to Connar's needs. So I decided she was creative, artistic, and a woman who when she fell in love, gave her heart forever.

Why would Dixie marry Connar, then run away? What if he was her childhood hero? She'd always loved him, so when he asked her to marry him, she naturally said yes. But for a vulnerable, creative person like Dixie, a girl who needed love, Connar's lifestyle could be impossible to handle.

I needed to know her prime motivating force. I needed a prime motivating event in Dixie's past that made her particularly vulnerable to Connar.

Then I had it. Her father was a television journalist who filled her childhood with broken promises. He skipped out on birthdays to attend wars on the other side of the world, canceled promised holidays to rush to the latest assassination. Because this would be particularly devastating if he were her only parent, I decided her mother had died at a young age.

If Dixie spent her childhood being disappointed by that sort of man, why marry one? Because people do exactly that, marry the image of the parent that gave them so much pain, subconsciously trying to get it right. Dixie had a dream rooted in her early childhood. As a young girl, she and her mother followed her father around the world, an adventurous period Dixie remembers as loving and happy. The adventure ended when her mother died and Dixie's father brought her to Canada to live with a paid foster mother. This life change was Dixie's prime motivating event. Her father made the first of many broken promises when he said he'd be back for Dixie's birthday.

Jessie was a single mother struggling to make it on a Gulf Island farm. Her son Connar thought of himself as an older brother to Dixie, but she worshipped him, dreaming that one day she would grow up and marry him. Connar had his own dream. I knew I was on the right track, because everything was falling into place. Connar never meant to marry at all. He didn't know who his father was, probably never would know because his mother wouldn't talk about it.

Dixie's father Devlin appeared in Connar's life when Conn was 13. He became Conn's hero, a man who lived adventure, appeared on television in exciting places doing exciting things. Devlin in turn seemed to care about Connar, and encouraged him to dream that he could follow Dev's footsteps.

2. Incompatible dreams

Connar grew up dreaming of an adventurous, free life where he would always be uncovering truth. And although he was attracted

> I needed to know Dixie's prime motivating force.

to Dixie as she grew into a woman, he had more important things to do than fall in love.

Dixie wanted to marry Connar, but she wanted him to be a family man, present for her in a way her father never was. Connar wanted to pursue truth and honesty out in the world.

My story required that she marry Connar impulsively, then leave just as impulsively. These were the actions of a young woman, perhaps not more than 19 or 20. But Dixie and Connar needed maturity to make the kind of compromises they would have to make to be happy together. At this point, I realized Dixie must have been gone for some years.

My hero must be in his mid-thirties, at that life stage where he's made a success of his career and begins to wonder if his original goals are all there is. As for my heroine, I wanted her to be a woman, not a girl. Connar was a complex man who would overwhelm a girl.

A man who has pursued his own dream to the exclusion of everyone else is a selfish man. He needs to be metaphorically hit over the head by a good heroine and shaken up to turn into a real hero. Dixie needed confidence and emotional strength to force him to see a few truths about himself.

I decided she was 27, had married him seven years ago and left almost immediately after the wedding. I wasn't sure why he had married her.

3. Going deeper

It's as important to know your characters' weaknesses as it is to know their strengths.

Why did Dixie run? Why did she still feel the urge to run after seven years? Why was Connar still determined to find her? What did he want from her? What motivated these people to get into this mess? What was Connar's weak spot? Dixie's? Why was their relationship messed up? What made these people behave in what looks like an irrational way?

People do act irrationally at times. Human beings are driven by emotion, complexes, and hang-ups. It's as important to know a character's weaknesses as his or her strengths.

What sort of person is Connar? He's determined to succeed despite having no father, a disability he never talks about. He's ambitious, has a hot temper he keeps under control — so he's passionate. He fights for what he believes in, a characteristic consistent with the type of journalist he is. He's impulsive, otherwise he wouldn't dive into danger for a story.

Under the aggressive man is still the boy who isn't sure of his origins, so roots are important to him. He believes a child should have a father and a mother, a "normal home," because he didn't have one. If a man like this has a child, there's no way he can be comfortable with anything less than a mommy-daddy-baby home for the kid.

I began playing with the idea of Dixie having Connar's baby without his knowledge. Dixie, I decided, is accompanied by a child. If Dixie was pregnant when she left Connar, the child would be six years old by this time.

If Connar's wife left him shortly after the wedding, and he doesn't know about the baby, what does he want from Dixie now? What if Connar doesn't know why Dixie had left and it's still driving him crazy after seven years? He is a newsman, a man driven to know *why*. He is also a man in his mid-thirties, disillusioned with his original dream that he can change the world as a truth-seeking newsman. I decided he's come home to write a book on television news, a book full of hard truths, and after the book is done he plans to negotiate for control of a TV news documentary show. He wants control of how the news is shown.

A truth-seeking man working on organizing the second half of his life, a man who hasn't enough roots for his own comfort. His wife left him seven years ago without any explanation. He doesn't know if she's alive or dead, and he doesn't know why she left. If he finds her alive he wants two things from her. An explanation and a divorce.

I turned to Dixie. Why did she leave Connar? I know she still loves him.

I looked to her weaknesses, her vulnerabilities. She loved her father, but always felt she came last in his life. She's always dreamed of Connar falling in love with her and asking her to marry him. But what if he didn't marry her for love? What if Devlin died from a terrorist's bullet while on a news assignment. To up the stakes, what if it happened on television with Dixie watching? What if Connar, now a newsman, was with Devlin as he died, and Dev made him promise to look after Dixie?

When Devlin died, Connar was a modern man with no plan to marry, but suppose he got home and found Dixie wouldn't let him look after her? He thought of her as a kid, believed she couldn't look after herself. But what about his mother, Dixie's foster mother? I decided the mother must be dead, otherwise Connar wouldn't feel Dixie was alone in the world after Devlin's death. So I killed off Jessie.

When he asked her to marry him, Connar was sexually attracted to Dixie, but had never followed up on it because he wouldn't feel comfortable having an affair with the girl who grew up in his home. After Dev's death, he decided Dixie was different than other women. She was used to being a newsman's daughter. She understood. They could marry, be pals, and have sex when he came home from the wars. As for Dixie fitting into his plan, he had no idea she was traumatized by her father's repeated abandonment.

When he asked her to marry him, 20-year-old Dixie assumed Connar loved her and her childhood dream had come true. He'd take her everywhere he went. They'd be together like her mom and dad before her mom died.

The day after the wedding, Dixie discovered Connar planned to leave her behind when he went back to Europe. On the heels of that betrayal, she discovered that he married her only to keep a promise to her father, a man who never kept his own promises.

Dixie couldn't face Connar once she knew this truth. She ran, leaving only a note saying it can't work. She knew Conn would look for her, that he'd be compulsive about keeping his promise to her father. So she hid herself well, ending up living just across the border in Mexico where she felt Conn could never trace her.

Before you write your characters' love story, develop their backstory.

What has Dixie been doing these past seven years? I liked the idea of her as an artist. She was in art school, I decided, when her father died. After she ran away, she stopped in San Diego where she met a disabled widow who lived in Mexico. When Dixie discovered she was pregnant, the widow offered Dixie room and board in return for living with her and helping her. Dixie moved to Mexico where she developed a reasonable income from her paintings over time. She now sells her paintings in a mall in San Diego, which is where I decided she would look across a crowd and see Connar.

That's the backstory.

4. What's my conflict?

With the backstory developed, I made the following notes regarding conflict.

- **Initial conflict:** Connar wants to resolve loose ends, to know why Dixie left. He also wants a home and family now. Dixie is afraid to face Connar, afraid she still loves him, afraid he'll take over when he finds out about the child.

- **Developing conflict:** Connar's desire to legitimize his marriage for his daughter is complicated by falling in love with Dixie; while Dixie, still in love with Connar, vows passionately never again to be the one left behind. She's unwilling to see that he's changed and, perhaps more important, she's changed.

Having developed my characters and conflict, I now completed filling out the manuscript data sheet for the novel and updated my book notes to reflect my understanding of the characters and their history. I decided to call the book *Yesterday's Vows*. (See Appendix 1 for the complete book notes of *Yesterday's Vows*.)

What about plot?

I knew that once Connar and Dixie met again, stimulus and response would result in the conflict elements I'd developed. At some point, this conflict would climax in a black moment when all seemed lost. I didn't know what the black moment would be, but I knew it would center on Dixie's fear of being the one left behind, vulnerable but unloved, and Connar's need to have things settled and to have a family for his daughter.

I began writing the first scene of the book.

Dixie enters the mall with arms full of her own paintings, sees Connar's head over the crowd, and runs. As I write, deep in Dixie's point of view, Dixie realizes she isn't a child any more, running won't work. She stops and calls the store where her paintings are displayed. Connar has found her; best to try to control their meeting.

Dixie agrees to meet Connar in a public park because she doesn't want him to know where she lives. When they meet, they'll react to each other. How they react will determine my plot. Through each stimulus and response, I know that the ending will find Connar, Dixie, and their daughter together.

13.

Writing the book

a. Keeping track of details

There are many ways to organize and keep track of details about your characters and story line as you write. Some writers keep extensive notes in a notebook using pen and paper, while others record important notes about characters and plot on flash cards which can be shuffled around as needed. I'd suggest you experiment with different methods until you find the one that works for you.

In the past, I've used both flash cards and notebooks, but here's how I work now:

Until I start writing the novel, I refer to my notes on computer, but when I start writing I print out my notes and prop them open on my desk, or tack them on my bulletin board. (See Appendix 1.)

The three things in my notes that I refer to the most as I write the book are the *manuscript data sheet,* the *time line,* and the *calendar.* I begin developing all three of these before I write the book, and keep them up to date as I'm writing.

The manuscript data sheet records basic physical details about hero and heroine, plus a brief summary of their personalities and conflict. In the early chapters, I glance at the data sheet frequently. I often change the characters' names, the setting, and my vision of the conflict.

Near my data sheet, on a bulletin board near my monitor, I often tack up pictures of hero and heroine I've found in magazines. I glance at them as I write about the characters. I find my bulletin board particularly important in the first few chapters when I'm setting up the characters and situation for the reader.

I started doing time lines for my books about eight years ago. My time line is a table in a computer file in which I record the important events in hero and heroine's life from scene one in the book, back to each character's birth. I calculate and record the age of each character for each event. I enter the year of the event, or the exact date if it's an important one, such as September 30, 1986, when Dixie watched her father killed by an assassin's bullet on television. Recently, I developed a computer program that does these age calculations and arranges my history table automatically.

The time line helps me orient myself in my characters' past. When I come to the scene where Dixie is remembering her father's death, a glance at the time line tells me it was 1986, that Dixie was 20 at the time, and Connar was 27. When I refer to Devlin's death, one glance at my time line tells me exactly what stage in their lives these people were at when it happened.

As I write the book, I continue to add to the time line. When I write that Dixie entered art school at the age of 17, I switch to my time line file and type the information in. At a glance, I see that Connar was 24 and still working for Continental News when Dixie entered art school.

I do a time line for every book I write because it pays off.

Most of this information may never get to the reader, but because I know it, I can write the book without being confused or constantly having to stop and gather or create new information. When I'm revising and want to check if I've got an event placed consistently in time, I need only one glance at my time line. If I decide to write a spin-off or sequel to the book later, the time line will enable me to create new character history without inconsistencies between the two books.

When I wrote *Yesterday's Vows,* I was intrigued by the handicapped woman who took Dixie in when she was alone and pregnant. I don't have a story for her yet, but one day I might. It will save me a lot of grief to look back at the notes for *Yesterday's Vows* and know exactly what I said about Sue when I wrote this book, and exactly which years she and Dixie lived together.

The third thing I keep up-to-date as I write is the calendar. When I start a book, I print out or photocopy a calendar for the relevant time period. Then I jot down on the calendar the major events in the book, and note in which chapter they occur. The calendar for *Yesterday's Vows* wasn't detailed, but noting on which day events occurred

A time line can keep track of your characters' histories.

saved me a lot of pain later. I may think I'll remember that chapter 1 occurred on May 8, and exactly two days later Dixie met Connar back at the mall again. The truth is, by the time I'm on chapter 8, I'm likely to be confused about which day it is. Then I'll have to spend an hour rereading chapters and jotting down the time sequence as I go. It's easier to do a calendar.

I also keep a chapter list as I write. I jot down the chapter number or name, the date of the chapter in story time, a brief note about events in the chapter, and the word count. Like the calendar, this saves time later when I'm trying to locate specific events in the manuscript. If Dixie remembers something Connar said on their wedding night, I can easily locate the wedding night scene by referring to the chapter list.

b. Stalling point

In *Yesterday's Vows,* I wrote chapters 1 to 4 with no problem.

- **Chapter 1:** Dixie sees Conn over the heads of the crowd, recognizes him and runs. She then stops at a pay phone, phones the gallery where she saw Conn looking at her pictures, and arranges to meet him later in a public place. I end the chapter with a brief visit to the hero's point of view, with Connar thinking of how he found Dixie, remembering seeing one of her paintings in his network chief's office.

- **Chapter 2:** Dixie meets Conn at Shelter Island, arriving by taxi so he won't see her Mexican license plates. He says he wants an explanation and a divorce. She evades explanation.

- **Chapter 3:** Flashback to Dixie's coming to Connar's home as a child. Chapter ends with memory of her father's death.

- **Chapter 4:** Flashback to Dixie's father's funeral and her marriage to Connar, on to the point where they are about to make love on the wedding night.

1. Brick wall

I was about to write chapter 5. I was back in the present with the story, and I had to do something about the baby Dixie had hidden from Connar. I spent a couple of days trying to write the chapter, finally realized it wasn't working, but had no idea what was wrong. I had to stop writing to get on a train to Chicago for a writer's conference. On the train, I spent some time talking to writer Kay Gregory who kindly offered herself as a sounding board.

Listening to myself talk, I decided that the baby was the problem. If Dixie had a baby, how would she ever know if Conn wanted her or the baby? I thought about the problems between Conn and Dixie and decided the baby was an unnecessary complication.

2. Remaining sensitive to characters

In writing a novel, it's important to remember that you are the storyteller, telling *your characters'* story. You'll probably have a picture of how story events will unfold as you write your book, but remember that it's important to let your characters develop naturally. It's essential that you remain sensitive to your characters and willing to let the story change from your original idea when your characters tell you it's necessary.

> It's essential that you remain sensitive to your characters.

Here's what happened to me as I was writing *Yesterday's Vows:*

I wrote chapter 5 en route to Chicago, writing a childless Dixie. After the conference, I continued writing on my portable computer on the trip home, revising chapters 1 to 4 to delete the baby from the story.

I was writing chapter 6 when my characters threw me a curve.

Dixie and Conn were in a San Diego park with Dixie's dog, Wolf. Dixie figured she wasn't in love with Connar any more, but Connar had just asked her to try to make a go of the marriage again. Then he kissed her and she was desperate to get her breath physically and emotionally. She needed to shove something between them.

I was typing fast, the words flowing.

> *"You haven't forgotten," he murmured. "Nothing's changed." He drew his mouth back from hers. He watched her face through heavy lidded eyes and she knew he saw her lips trying to follow his to bring him back — her body voting without permission from her mind. "You'll come back to me," he said. "You want this as much as I do."*
>
> *His mouth came towards her again and she felt the air go out of her lungs in a long stream. "Connar, stop! I —"*
>
> *He paused with his lips a heartbeat away from hers. He touched her mouth with his fingers and traced the shape of her lips. "Is that really what you want? Do you want me to stop? To leave you alone?" His fingers touched the slight parting of her lips and coaxed a caress from her mouth, then his mouth moved to take hers and she knew she had no strength to pull away.*
>
> *"There's a child," she said desperately. "Your child."*

What's going on here? Dixie, didn't you and I agree that we didn't need a baby?

Obviously, I agreed, but Dixie didn't. After this many books, if I'd learned anything it was that I wasn't writing this story. Dixie and Connar were. I was just the storyteller.

From this point on, the story wrote itself in a sequence of stimulus and response transactions. Once Connar knew about the child, he insisted on meeting his daughter, Jessie, who Dixie had named after Conn's own mother. Dixie took Conn to meet Jess. Conn, accustomed to manipulating others, pressured Dixie to bring Jess to his home on Thetis Island so he could get to know his daughter. Nervous of losing Jess to Conn, Dixie insisted on coming too. Once on his own territory, Conn initiated a campaign to win his daughter and his estranged wife. Dixie resented the manipulation, and feared becoming vulnerable to Connar again.

Conn manipulated Dixie through Jess, motivated by his love of both his daughter and his wife, and his fear Dixie would leave him again. Dixie distrusted Conn because he'd once planned to leave her behind just as her father had. When Conn won his daughter over to the point she burst into tears at the suggestion they might leave his home, Dixie knew she must break away before she was completely unable to protect herself from hurt.

Dixie's decision to leave created the black moment.

The purpose of a black moment in a story is to shake the characters up, make them realize what they risk losing, and what really matters. In *Yesterday's Vows*, the black moment made Dixie see that she was no longer the inexperienced girl who'd married Conn, that if she lived with him now she'd be a different person. She saw that he had changed too, that he truly loved their daughter. For Conn, the black moment made him realize he cared about Dixie enough to risk opening up and showing her how much he loved her.

With both Conn and Dixie determined to salvage their relationship if at all possible, the last scene naturally resulted in a happy ending.

3. Everything is disposable

One of the most important things to remember in storytelling is that anything in your story can be changed. When you send your book to a publisher, you may find the editor has ideas for improving your novel. Be flexible. Remember, your objective is to tell your romantic story in the most effective way possible. Your characters' actions aren't cast in stone. Take a new, critical look at your story. Is the

> **Remember: Anything in your story can be changed. Everything is disposable.**

editor right? if you're not sure, try doing the revisions and see if it improves your story.

When I sent *Yesterday's Vows* to my editor, she said she loved the story, but asked, "Don't you think it might be better to start at chapter 2 with Dixie on her way to meet Connar at Shelter Island?"

I sat down with the manuscript and started reading from chapter two, the scene after the market scene. My editor was right. I filtered the essentials from chapter 1 into Dixie's thoughts in chapter 2, and threw out the rest of the chapter. Because I'd originally envisioned that she-sees-him/she-runs scene as a perfect opening, I'd hung onto it and failed to see that the next scene made a better starting point.

c. Story sparks

Some time ago I realized that I'd written another story that could have come from this same spark. *Hidden Memories* opens with the heroine recognizing the hero across a crowd in an art gallery, and panicking. The heroine of *Hidden Memories* runs emotionally more than physically, but the basic spark is the same. Yet the stories are so different I didn't realize they came from the same origin until a year after I wrote *Yesterday's Vows*.

I could easily write another romance novel, this time with the woman really in a Mexican market. It would also be a different story. What makes a story unique is not the plot device that gets it started; but the characters, their conflict, and the voice of the writer.

Part 4

Developing power in your writing

14.

A unique voice and picture for each character

a. The need to know who's talking

> Voice #1: *"I always thought you'd leave one day. I had a feeling, from the beginning."*
>
> Voice #2: *"You always knew I'd leave? Why would I leave?"*

Which voice is the heroine? Which the hero?

Ideally, your dialogue itself should tell the reader who's speaking, with the minimum use of "he said" and "she said." Each character should have his or her own voice, just as each of your acquaintances has a unique way of phrasing comments.

Take a notebook and go out to a coffeehouse. Get a cup of cappuccino or a latté, then sit and open your ears to the conversations around you. Pull out your pen and jot down phrases. Notice how the teenage girl's words and phrases differ from the middle-aged man's. When you've filled your page with scraps of conversation, go to a baseball game and take more notes. Sit on a bus and record the driver's unique way of speaking. Notice how the poet's conversation differs from the farmer's.

Return to your own romance novel and examine your dialogue. Does the heroine's teenage daughter speak like a teenager? What sort of teenager? A bookworm? The life of the party? Find a teenager to use as a model, listen to how she talks. Would your character speak like this?

b. Speech patterns

Think of speech patterns in the same way as a character's personal history or the details of his or her job. You need to show the reader each character's unique voice, without overdoing it.

> *So I — like you know what I mean. I told him — I asked him like did he have to always — like you know what I mean — every time he has to go and answer the door. Like you know what I mean. He's answering the door and like you know what I mean. Like it bugs me.*

Real-life speech is sprinkled with empty words and phrases: like, you know what I mean, okay, ah, eh. Most of us use and hear these empty words so often that our ears filter them out.

When portraying a character's unique speech, hint at repetitive patterns, don't reproduce them exactly.

When you're portraying a character's unique speech, hint at these repetitive patterns, don't reproduce them exactly. If the speaker you're using for a model says "like you know what I mean" several times in a five-minute period, you can get the feel of her conversation by using the phrase once.

> *So I told him, I asked him. Like did he have to always — every time he has to go and answer the door. Like you know what I mean. He's answering the door and like it bugs me.*

In the second version of the above example, I used the empty phrase "like you know what I mean" only once, but I used the word "like" three times. How often you use a characteristic empty word or phrase is something you'll need to judge for yourself. Reread each dialogue passage to determine the balance where each character's words seem natural. When I wrote the passage above, I had in mind a teenage girl complaining about her father. Initially I stripped out all but one instance of "like," but the dialogue sounded stilted for a teenager, so I put two back in.

If I were to write a response to the teenager's complaint, I'd phrase it to indicate the speaker. If the second person was the girl's mother, I might write,

> *Why are you always so touchy? He's your father. He deserves your respect.*

If it were a girlfriend, she'd respond with different words, different content.

If every character has the same verbal voice, the reader won't have a sense of who's speaking. Even when there's no speech, the reader needs a sense of who the viewpoint character is. You can achieve this through your character's silent voice — thoughts —and through actions and body language.

c. Voice: Verbal and non-verbal

Dialogue is made up of both verbal and non-verbal communication. When you're talking with a woman friend who says, "I don't care what time he gets home," you may notice that her voice sounds brittle and her fists are clenched. While you hear the message of her words — she doesn't care — you also see the tension of her body and know she *does* care.

Body language is so much a part of our communication; we often send and receive body signals unconsciously. We signal disapproval with our faces and our bodies, with eye contact or lack of it. We signal anger, love, intimacy, rejection. We mark territorial boundaries.

Your characters first learned body language in childhood. Perhaps your heroine's parents were an inhibited middle-class mother and a blue-collar father of Scottish descent. Neither spoke of emotions. Feelings were communicated by body language only. Your heroine became expert in sending and reading body language, while developing a speech style that denied feelings. If her husband came home late, she'd say she didn't care while her body radiated tension.

When you write your characters' dialogue, reveal their true feelings through body language. Sometimes, the words and body language contradict each other. Your readers will subconsciously analyze the combination and draw their own conclusions about your characters.

1. Showing emotion with body language

> *She telephoned Charles from Crescent City…When the call rang through she almost hung up before the second ring.*
>
> *His answering machine would answer. She did not know if she would talk to the machine…*
>
> *A woman answered.*
>
> *Carrie dropped the receiver.*

In this passage from *After All This Time*, I don't say Carrie was upset when a woman answered. Carrie's action of dropping the receiver without speaking is a body language signal the reader will recognize. Whenever you can, show signs of your character's

Your characters first learned body language in childhood.

Reveal your characters' true feelings through body language.

A UNIQUE VOICE AND PICTURE FOR EACH CHARACTER

emotions. It's more powerful than telling your reader what the character feels.

2. Studying body language

Many beginning writers give all their characters the same voice and the same body language. Looking back on my own earliest books, I see that my hero and heroine often spoke with the same wordiness, the same phrasing, the same emotional content. They "shrugged" and "grinned" frequently, while I tried to find other actions for them.

To enrich your body language vocabulary, begin studying people. Go back to that coffeehouse with your notebook. Watch the woman who sits with arms crossed protectively and talks rapidly to her companion, never making eye contact. What does her body language tell you about her? Whether you're right or wrong, your speculations could form the basis of a fascinating character.

If you're in a relationship, listen as you talk to your partner. Listen to your partner's responses. Who is more verbal? How much communication is non-verbal?

Read books such as Julius Fast's *Body Language* to heighten your awareness. Think about the factors that influence speech, thought patterns, and body language. Think about your characters. What body language did they learn from parents or childhood playmates? What body language have they learned at college?

How have your characters deliberately changed body language as adults? A woman may walk more aggressively to be safer on the streets. What deliberate changes to your body language have you made as an adult?

d. Men, women, and brain sex

Men and women generally move differently, speak differently, and think differently. As a writer, you don't need to know whether these differences are genetic, cultural, or social, as long as your characters act, speak, and think in a manner consistent with their background, their genetics, and their gender.

1. Men should talk like men

I wrote *Pacific Disturbance* in the early 1980s. Now, I find many things wrong with it. When Max remembers aloud how Lucy first approached him asking for a job, he says:

> Your characters should act, speak, and think in a manner consistent with their background, their genetics, and their gender.

Ever since you started working at SCS, I've been thankful you didn't let me send you away. These last few months we've accomplished more than I ever dreamed possible. We work well together." He reached across the table and touched her hand. "I believe in hanging on to my friends, too. We are friends, aren't we, Lucy?"

I now believe this dialogue sounds more like a woman's speech than a man's. I think most men would be more likely to say, "You're doing okay. I'm glad I hired you." Brief, succinct, no wasted words.

Men and women speak differently. When Max says, "We are friends, aren't we?" he's not speaking like a typical man. On average, men don't spend a lot of words on emotions. Men say a few words, a hint. Women read meanings into those words. He says, "You did okay." She translates it to mean she did a wonderful job. He takes out the garbage. She translates the action into the words, "I love you."

Women fill in the blanks men leave when they talk.

Unless your hero has a background that has trained him to speak comfortably about his feelings, perhaps as a counselor or psychologist, he's unlikely to be as comfortable talking about feelings as your heroine. When he does, he'll state his thoughts in concrete terms, more briefly than she would.

Look back at the dialogue between hero and heroine at the beginning of this chapter. Both voice #1 and voice #2 express feelings. Both use extra, non-essential words and repetition to express their thoughts.

By making the hero's speech more masculine (briefer, more concrete, with less feeling content) than the heroine's, I can give the reader a sense of who's talking. To make absolutely certain the reader knows who's talking, I can use a speech tag (in this case, "she whispered") on one of the character's dialogue lines. Because the hero's terse words will be empty of feeling, I'll use body language to indicate his suppressed emotion. Note in the passage below, from my book *After All This Time,* how the heroine's words show repetition and reveal her confusion, while the hero's words focus on concrete details. Even when he talks about believing she would leave, he says "I always knew," not "I thought" or "I believed."

"I always knew you'd leave one day."

She whispered, "What? You always knew I'd leave? Why would I leave?"

"Inevitable." He pushed his hand into his pocket. "I'm no fool, Carrie. It was inevitable that, once you realized

you could make it on your own, you'd want to try." His
voice was slow, casual, but his jaw jerked, the single sign
of tension.

2. Gender differences

Each man and woman is unique, but there are common traits most men exhibit, and common traits women exhibit. Understanding these helps us create more realistic characters and more powerful love stories.

For more information on common differences between the speech and thoughts of men and women, read *Men Are from Mars, Women Are from Venus*, by John Gray.

3. Men and women in love

John Gray says men and women approach problems differently. When a man has a problem, he withdraws, going "into his cave" to solve it by himself. A woman wants to talk her problem out. This men-withdraw/women-talk pattern is common between the sexes, although not universal.

If your hero has a problem, he'll probably go off to solve it himself. He'll be unlikely, or unwilling to talk about his problem before he's worked out the solution. If your heroine has a problem, she'll want to talk about it, share her feelings. If hero and heroine have the same problem, he'll withdraw to work it out. She may try to follow him, to talk about it. If she does, he'll withdraw further, which she'll interpret as rejection.

Does he love me? Doesn't he love me? The question torments both heroines and real women. Part of the reason it's such a problem is that men and women have different value systems, different goals, different communication styles. Perhaps we do come from different planets.

4. Keeping score

Gray claims men and women keep score differently. A woman believes every indication of love is worth one point. A man believes signs of love get points according to their importance. Think about the relationships you know and decide whether you believe this is true.

If men and women score differently, it's no wonder heroes and heroines have difficulty resolving the love problem.

The hero makes a big, non-verbal gesture of love. He takes the heroine to Paris for the weekend. He thinks he's told her he loves her

> If men and women keep score differently, it's no wonder heroes and heroines have difficulty resolving the love problem.

without words by giving her a 30-point vacation. He doesn't know she expects him to keep on saying it, to say it in words and get more points. She's sitting there thinking, okay, he took me to Paris for a week, but I haven't had a call from him in the last four days. He's scored only one point. He doesn't really care. Meanwhile, the hero is at work getting the money to pay for another Paris trip, figuring he's ahead on the score and will soon have another 30 points. The poor hero doesn't get it that she'd score him more points if he spent five minutes a day calling her to say he misses her, than taking her to Paris every blue moon.

Even though this hero is a Martian, if he comes to understand that his Venusian heroine has this crazy scoring system, he'll go out of his way to say "I love you" and even pick up his socks, although it doesn't make sense to him. Because he realizes the heroine needs all those little scores to feel loved. Because he loves her.

5. Different how?

Scientists have put babies in front of a TV screen and given them a string to pull, to switch the picture. Both boys and girls quickly learned to pull the string to get a new picture. When the switch was disconnected, the boys kept pulling harder and harder. The girls got upset and gave up.

Boys get obstinate when things go wrong; girls get upset, often give up and try something else. Stubbornness or determination, whatever you call it, males are born with more of it. Therefore, the thoughts and speech of your heroes should generally show them to be more stubborn than your heroines. When your heroine is stubborn, your hero may not be expecting it.

Boys inhabit a world of things and space. They are better at imagining things in three dimensions, judging distance and perspective. They tend to be better mathematicians, better navigators, better mechanics. After testing over a million kids, scientists have found that in the top one percent of math students, there are 130 boys for every 10 girls.

Generally, heroes will be better mechanics and mathematicians than testosterone-deprived heroines. If you create a heroine outstanding in these skills, be sure to balance that strength with other, female strengths. You want your reader to realize that your math-loving heroine isn't just a man wearing woman's clothes.

Girls inhabit a world of sounds and words. They learn to talk and read earlier than boys. Through life, girls are better at communicating,

A UNIQUE VOICE AND PICTURE FOR EACH CHARACTER

better at reading, and better at listening, although studies report that men of the nineties are better at communicating than men of the seventies were.

Are your heroines better at reading, listening, and communicating than your heroes? Science has found women are physically better equipped to communicate. They have language functions in both the left and right sides of the brain, but men have language functions in the left only. Thus women talk and listen about feelings and problems easier than men. Men are more silent.

6. Brain sex implications for writers

A few years ago, I wrote *After All This Time*. When the hero told the heroine he was pleased with her work, he did it differently than Max in *Pacific Disturbance*.

> *She quickly discovered that as an employer Charles was demanding, quietly arrogant, and endlessly exciting. He terrified Carrie by constantly giving her more and more responsibility. When she made a mistake he criticized her mercilessly, then promptly gave her another chance.*

Although Charles was pleased with Carrie's work, he didn't say, "Carrie, I'm really glad I hired you. You're doing a great job." Instead, he gave her harder work to do. As an intuitive woman, Carrie understood.

In *Pacific Disturbance*, my first novel, Lucy worked for Max, then ran away from him to escape his sexual pursuit of her. In *After All This Time*, my twenty-first book, Carrie ran away from her employer, Charles, after making the mistake of going to bed with him after five years in his employ. Both men followed their runaway women. Whether they knew it or not, I knew each was in love with the heroine he pursued.

With almost ten years between the writing of Max and Charles, I learned more about portraying men, and dealt with the confrontation scenes differently.

When Max caught up with Lucy, he said:

> *I wondered if it was you. I saw the name on the door —*
> *L. Carter, Certified General Accountant. It had to be you.*

A moment later, he said,

> *I didn't expect that you would just disappear. When I left you in your apartment that night, I knew we had problems to work out, but you didn't stay to work them out. You ran.*

If I were writing *Pacific Disturbance* today, I'd handle the whole scene differently because I now understand most men are more comfortable acting than talking.

In *After All This Time,* when Charles tracked Carrie down in Mexico, he said simply, "I want to talk to you." And she thought, "Alone. He wanted to see her alone."

Carrie read the extra meaning into Charles' words.

In *After All This Time,* Carrie is usually the one doing the talking. Her nervousness is translated into speech. When men are nervous, they don't blabber; they withdraw. Women talk.

When Charles does get Carrie alone, he doesn't go into a speculation of why she left, or, like Max, a rehash of finding her gone. Instead, he says, "I've come to take you back. I have no intention of letting you leave me right now."

Some men would be briefer, saying only, "You're coming with me," but I'd endowed Charles with a veneer of civilization over the cave man, so he added a few words to soften the command.

When a reader reads a story about men and women reacting to each other in familiar ways, she believes in the characters' motivation and behavior because they are familiar to her. Most women can understand why a heroine would doubt the love of a silent man who won't talk about his feelings. Most women can understand why a heroine would feel angry when the man she loves says, "You're coming with me," without explaining or apologizing for yesterday's argument.

7. Intimacy for men and women

Men derive intimacy from doing things together. The term "male bonding" usually refers to two men feeling close through sharing an activity such as fixing a car. Women derive intimacy from talking about feelings. When you want your hero and heroine to share an intimate period, have them do something while they talk.

> When you want your hero and heroine to share an intimate period, have them do something while they talk.

In *Pacific Disturbance,* my heroine told my hero about her unhappy previous marriage for eight pages while they stood together, motionless. His only action was to touch her face. If I were writing that scene now, I'd have more action and I'd cut the hero's dialogue to a minimum, eliminating passages like this, from Max:

> *You've had a bereavement, too, Lucy. You have to let yourself heal. You lost your parents, then you lost your husband. The man you fell in love with didn't exist. He was*

115 ❦

> *your hope for security and your dream of love..., so the*
> *disillusionment you suffered was as great a bereavement*
> *as any loss from death."*

Sympathy from a man is every bit as genuine as sympathy from a woman, but it's rarely as wordy. He's not likely to stand at the end of a path or sit behind a desk for seven pages without doing something physical while they talk.

When I wrote *After All This Time*, my hero and heroine still talked, but if Charles had to stand still while talking, he fidgeted.

> *He pushed his hand into his pocket. Again she heard the*
> *movement of coins. Upstairs she heard Allie's voice raised*
> *in protest. She said, "You need a pencil."*
>
> *"What?"*
>
> *"A pencil to fool with. You always do that when*
> *you're angry."*

e. Other factors that distinguish characters

1. Occupation

In *After All This Time*, my hero is an entrepreneur, accustomed to using dialogue to persuade others to his will. If he were a fisher or a mechanic, more accustomed to working with his hands than his voice, I'd write his body language differently.

> *"I always figured you'd leave."*
>
> *She whispered, "What? You knew I'd leave? Why would*
> *I leave?"*
>
> *"Because." He shoved his hand into his jeans pocket.*
> *"Sooner or later I knew you'd figure out you didn't need*
> *me." His voice was harsh, cold, and his jaw jerked as he*
> *stopped speaking.*

If he were a counselor, I might write him like this:

> *"I always knew you'd leave one day."*
>
> *She whispered, "What? You always knew I'd leave?*
> *Why would I leave?"*
>
> *"Because of who you are." He pushed his hand into his*
> *pocket. "I know you, Carrie. You've always needed to*
> *prove to yourself that you can do everything on your own.*
> *It was inevitable you'd think of leaving once you got*
> *enough confidence." His voice was slow, casual, but his*
> *jaw jerked, the single sign of tension.*

Brain Sex: Science's Contribution to Your Characters

1. Brain scans show men have to work harder to distinguish facial expressions than women do. Remember when you're writing, most men don't see facial indications of emotion as readily as women.

2. The membrane that connects left and right brain hemispheres is reportedly larger in women than men. Many scientists believe women integrate information from all senses better than men. If so, your heroine will be more intuitive than your hero, better able to make many connections, to concentrate on many things at the same time.

3. Men are better at focusing exclusively on one thing. A survival trait: if the hero is distracted on his hunting trip, the buffalo will get away and his family will starve.

4. Scientists have found men's hearing starts off worse than women's from birth. You don't have to make your hero hearing impaired, but realize that he probably won't hear everything the heroine says. Men have a harder time hearing some sounds than women. She thinks he's tuning out, doesn't want to hear what she's saying. In fact, he's having trouble hearing what she's saying.

5. Men derive intimacy from doing things with women. Women derive intimacy from talking. The most popular dates are activities where doing is combined with talking. On a dinner date, hero and heroine *do eating* together. At a night club, they *do drinking and dancing.* On a hike, they *do walking.* A hero who is comfortable talking for a long period of time without activity may seem unreal.

6. Men are more promiscuous than women. Men expect sex earlier in a relationship than women do.

7. Women like talk. Men like things and sex. In courting, each tries to please the other. Men court women with words, while women court men with sexy clothing. When courting, your hero will become more verbal to please the heroine, while your heroine will dress and make up her face to attract his desire for sex even if she doesn't plan to go to bed with him. It's an instinctive response to the stirring of love, as old as the cave people.

8. In a group, studies show a man tends to focus on who's boss. A woman tends to focus on keeping everyone in the group content and functioning.

2. Relationships and roles

As people, we behave differently with our lovers than with our children, our coworkers, our bosses, our employees, or our parents. We modify behavior to suit the relationship. In the above example from *After All This Time,* Charles and Carrie have two relationships: one as lovers and the other as employer-employee. For both Charles and Carrie, how they behave with a lover is different than how they behave with an employer or employee. The coexistence of these two relationships creates a conflict within both Charles and Carrie, a need to make a choice between the behavior suited to lovers, and that suited to employee-employer.

Look at the passage again:

"I always knew you'd leave one day."

She whispered, "What? You always knew I'd leave? Why would I leave?"

"Inevitable." He pushed his hand into his pocket. "I'm no fool, Carrie. It was inevitable that, once you realized you could make it on your own, you'd want to try." His voice was slow, casual, but his jaw jerked, the single sign of tension.

Charles is speaking as Carrie's employer, but although his dialogue contains no reference to Carrie as his lover, his body language — the jerking of his jaw — reveals the conflict. It's the lover whose jaw is jerking, revealing tension.

On the other hand, Carrie is caught in her recent role as Charles' lover. As his employee, she's normally rational, cool, and non-emotional. In the above passage, she's confused and disoriented, unable to anchor herself in the role of competent employee. Her whispering reflects uncertainty and vulnerability. Her confusion is revealed when she repeats words and concepts: "What? You always knew I'd leave? Why would I leave?"

How will your characters' changing relationship roles affect their speech and actions?

As your story progresses, your characters' relationships will change. As a new relationship evolves, it's bound to cause inner conflict for your characters. How will your characters' changing relationship roles affect their speech and actions? What are your characters trying to hide? How will their hidden emotions show in body language?

3. Culture and education

If a character is educated to different patterns of speech and behavior than those he or she grew up with, dialogue and body language, may change. But when that character is under stress, he or she is likely to revert to old patterns. Regardless of training, some hint of a character's earliest influences will always remain.

In *Catalina's Lover*, my hero was born into a family of Peruvian landowners. Juan grew up with Spanish as his first language. His family were upper-class landowners, rulers of the peasant class. He learned English at an early age, being educated in the United States and England. Although Juan's English was fluent, I was careful to remember that his first language was Spanish. I showed this by retaining some Spanish structures to his speech even when he was speaking English. I made his speech slightly more grammatical and less colloquial than my heroine's. When he was angry or emotional, I gave his speech and body language more of a macho, dominating flavor than at other times, because Juan was born into a culture where *machismo* is highly valued.

As you write your characters, focus on what you know of their culture and education. Reveal hints of background in actions and words, but be careful not to overdo characteristic regional speaking patterns.

4. Behavior and emotional state

Each of your characters will act and talk in different ways at different times. Most people behave differently when they are calm than when they're emotionally aroused. Think about your hero and heroine. You know how they act and talk normally, how they choose to behave. You've looked at the relationships in their lives and you know how your hero behaves to his sister, his mother, and his boss. You know what his self-concept dictates.

You also need to know how your character will behave when uncontrollable emotions overwhelm. You're writing a love story. Sooner or later both hero and heroine must give way to uncontrollable emotions, and they'll probably be frightened by these emotions. When frightening emotions take over, most people revert to behavior patterns from their youth.

When the civilized hero Juan from *Catalina's Lover* is unwillingly overwhelmed by his love for Cathy, he becomes more a Spanish conquistador and less a civilized man: more domineering, more jealous, more demanding, and less sensitive to Cathy's emotional needs and fears. As Cathy's feelings for Juan threaten to get out of control, Cathy loses her veneer of calm sophistication, her world-traveler confidence. Her reactions to Juan became more emotional and less rational.

> When your characters fall in love, the way they act and speak to each other will change.

When your characters fall in love, the way they act and speak to each other will change. Their vulnerability will cause them to lose their customary mask of behavior, to react more emotionally, with less conscious control of their words and actions.

119

15.

Sensuality in your love story

Whether your hero and heroine make love in the pages of your novel will depend on your own level of comfort with writing love scenes, on the story you are writing and where it fits in the marketplace, and on the characters themselves.

Even if you and your characters decide that hero and heroine will share nothing more than a kiss between the covers of your novel, you must show your readers the chemistry, the mutual need, and the compulsion to intimacy that distinguishes lovers from best friends. Even a virginal heroine must be aware that marriage and life partnership with the hero will mean physical intimacy. The reader needs to know the heroine wants the hero to make love to her; while the hero desires her above all other women, loving her enough to remain faithful throughout their lives.

Romance heroines of the early 1960s did not make love with heroes except in marriage, and even then the act was not described in the book. Nevertheless, those romance novels sizzled with romantic tension. Writers such as Mary Burchell and Jane Donnelly were experts at creating intense levels of sexual tension without hero and heroine sharing more than a powerful kiss.

Because romance novels have changed to reflect women's changing view of themselves, many heroines of today choose to make love within the covers of the romance novel. Many readers prefer hero and heroine to consummate their relationship in the book. Others want a chaste, romantic story.

Most romance publishers have editorial guidelines for writers, giving a brief outline of the sort of story they judge suitable for each

Many heroines of today choose to make love within the covers of the romance novel.

of the publisher's imprints. These guidelines generally include a reference to the level of sensuality readers are accustomed to seeing in each line. For sample editorial guidelines, see chapter 22.

a. A sensuality level for every taste

Whatever level of sensuality you feel comfortable writing, there's probably a place for your book in today's market.

1. The inspirational romance

In these romances, hero and heroine achieve a strong spiritual intimacy with each other and their higher power. The books are highly romantic, but characters do not make love in the book.

2. The traditional romance

Romantic and heartwarming, these stories focus on traditional values and the growth of strong romantic feelings between hero and heroine. Harlequin's editorial guidelines for their Romance line state, "the emphasis should be on warm and tender emotions, with no sexual explicitness; lovemaking should only take place when the emotional commitment between the characters justifies it." For Silhouette Romance, the guidelines specify, "Although the hero and heroine don't actually make love unless married, sexual tension is a vitally important element."

3. Contemporary romance — appropriate sensuality

These novels feature modern men and women with high ethics. Writers are generally free to find the level of sensuality that suits them, their story, and their characters. Publishers' editorial guidelines usually contain phrases such as "whether the sensuality is sizzling or subtle" (Silhouette Special Edition) or "a developing romance which may include explicit lovemaking" (Harlequin Presents). When characters make love, it is a natural outgrowth of the plot and the relationship.

4. Contemporary romance — high sensuality

In the last two decades, the sensual contemporary novel has gained in popularity. These novels often have red covers featuring hero and heroine in an embrace that suggests lovemaking is taking place, or is about to take place. Editorial guidelines generally specify sensuality as an essential part of these stories. Harlequin Temptation is described as "Harlequin's boldest, most sensuous series, focusing on men and women living — and loving — in the 1990s." These stories feature lovemaking, but as the editorial guidelines for Silhouette Desire state, "lovemaking is never taken lightly." The most successful novels focus on *lovemaking,* not sex.

5. Other worlds, other times

Many novels are set in other time periods — past or future. Some science fiction romances are set in other worlds. As in present day romances, sensuality in these books is sometimes expressed in lovemaking, and sometimes not. Many historical novels are highly sensual. On the other hand, many Regency historical novels follow the pattern of the famous author Georgette Heyer, portraying virginal heroines, protective heroes, and no explicit lovemaking. Publishers of novels set in other time periods don't always have editorial guidelines, but you can form an accurate picture of what's commonly acceptable by reading the latest offerings from the publisher you're thinking of sending your novel to.

6. The romantic intrigue

In making love, characters must allow both emotional and physical intimacy. They must become vulnerable to each other. In romantic intrigue, vulnerability may have risks beyond the danger of the emotional pain of unrequited love. The heroine is often in danger from the villain. She may not know who the villain is. Where there is an element of doubt about whether the hero is in fact the villain, it's probably inappropriate for the heroine to make love with the hero. A heroine may be foolish and impulsive, but readers become annoyed if she's blatantly stupid.

Another factor that often keeps lovemaking off the pages of romantic intrigue is the constant danger facing hero and heroine. When characters are fighting for survival, there's little opportunity for lovemaking. As in the contemporary romance, lovemaking in an intrigue should occur only when it grows naturally out of the characters and the situation.

7. Your novel

Write a romance you would enjoy reading. If you like sensual romances, but feel you can't write a love scene, give yourself a chance anyway. Writing a good love scene is no more difficult than writing any other scene if you remember:

- Every character action must be well motivated.

> Lovemaking should occur only when it grows naturally out of the characters and the situation.

- Everything in your novel must further the objective of your story.

- Your job is to show the reader what your characters are feeling.

b. Well-motivated lovers

Your reader may have had a hard day at the office. She may be exhausted from tending the needs of three young children. Your romance novel gives her the emotional release she needs, while affirming the basic dream that she can have and hold an intimate and powerful partnership with a lifetime lover — that she can walk hand and hand through life without ever having to be completely alone again.

Although your reader is more than willing to enter your fantasy world, nothing can cause the fantasy to crumble quicker than a dead love scene. If you put lovemaking into your book only because you believe it's necessary, it's likely to read like the token sex it is. Your hero, your heroine, and your reader will be disappointed.

1. Why make love?

Sexual attraction is a common event in adult life. Any one of us may feel stirrings of sexual desire on seeing an attractive individual of the opposite sex. We find a variety of sights, sounds, and touches sensual: the sway of a woman's hips, the deep huskiness of a man's voice, the smile we believe is seductive. We are stimulated sexually by touches, sounds, sights, and by our own imaginations. Writer Naomi Horton describes sexual tension as the conflict between "want" and "can't have." When your characters' hormones signal "want," remember that most people are accustomed to saying "can't have."

A man drives past a beautiful stranger and feels stirrings of desire. He continues down the street and goes on with his day. A woman watches her favorite actor making love on screen. She's aroused while realizing she can't herself make love with the actor. A man feels attracted to his best friend's wife. He suppresses the attraction and asks a coworker for a date.

If your hero and heroine make love simply to scratch a sexual itch, if you haven't given your reader reason to believe in these people and their lovemaking, you risk your reader tossing the book aside for another.

If your hero and heroine make love simply to scratch a sexual itch, you risk your reader tossing the book aside for another.

2. Choosing physical intimacy

When your hero and heroine first meet, they may feel a heightened awareness of each other that's unusual for both of them. In *With Strings Attached*, Molly first sees Patrick when he parks his car behind hers in the ferry lineup.

> *There was another vehicle behind hers now, a white classic Corvette with its convertible top down. Molly felt increasingly aware of the man at the wheel as she crossed the pavement towards her own vehicle. Just the two of them, alone in the ferry queue. Would she eventually come to know who he was? Would she learn all the islanders by name?*

The next time Molly sees Patrick, he's just accused her of trying to break into his neighbor's cabin. Although angry at the accusation, she is increasingly aware of him.

Earlier, when he had been sitting in his sports car, Molly had thought that he looked civilized and sexy. Here, with his clothing rumpled and that black hair tumbling down over his forehead, he looked more dangerous than the bears she had fantasized out there in the bushes.

As a young woman who has always avoided intimacy, Molly sees her sexual attraction to Patrick as dangerous. She feels desire, but because she fears emotional vulnerability, she fights her own feelings. She wants Patrick, but has no intention of giving in. But because this man is different in some way she can't define, Molly's normal barriers aren't effective. Instead of subsiding, her attraction intensifies.

> *"You feel it, don't you, Molly? This pull between us?"*
>
> *"Yes," she whispered. Was she insane, believing this man to be her fate? Wanting it to be true?*
>
> *A muscle worked at his temple. "Do I have time to go slow, Molly? How long are you staying on Gabriola?"*
>
> *Forever. Her lips parted to say the word, but Molly knew better than to believe in forever. She gulped and asked, "What do you want from me?"*

Because of her deep emotional wariness, Molly will fall in love only with a man she can trust completely. Even though she believes she can never be Patrick's life partner because of who she is, Molly comes to trust him with her vulnerability. Because Patrick is exactly the sort of man Molly can trust, when he realizes Molly wants him to slow down, he suppresses his own desires. Molly and Patrick are both saying "can't have" to their sexual "want" impulses — Molly because she's afraid of being hurt and Patrick because he cares about Molly's feelings.

The conflict between desire and the fear of intimacy intensifies all other conflicts in the story. It puts both hero and heroine on edge, complicating every interaction between them with the flavor of unsatisfied desires. Because Patrick and Molly have strong reasons to deny their desires, the reader understands the need for delaying lovemaking.

When the consummation of lovers is delayed, tension and suspense are often heightened. When hero and heroine are on the edge of making love, a child may come home unexpectedly. The telephone may ring. These events can heighten desire and frustration in the same way they would in real life, enhancing your novel. But if overdone, meaningless interruptions irritate the reader.

> When the consummation of lovers is delayed, tension and suspense are heightened — but don't overdo it!

If your characters have been fighting against building desire, eventually there comes a time when lovemaking is inevitable.

In *With Strings Attached,* Molly's growing desire and emotional intimacy with Patrick finally overcome her need for safety. Although she still believes she'll be hurt in an intimate relationship with a lover, she decides to become Patrick's lover.

> *"Molly, will you stay with me tonight?"*
>
> *She shivered. He had touched her until she was trembling and aching, whispering his name, almost begging him to love her. Then he had stepped back, when she wanted only to drown in his arms. The harshness in his moonlit face frightened her now. It would end with pain. She knew that, but she whispered, "Yes. I'll stay with you tonight."*

Like Molly, the characters in your romance novel may reach a point where the balance tips between desire and denial. Motivation for lovemaking becomes more powerful than the reasons for saying "can't have," and the characters choose to become lovers. On the other hand, your characters may be swept up in events that seem beyond their control.

3. Swept away by passion

Like Molly, many of my heroines have made the journey toward physical intimacy in progressive steps as the relationship developed. Generally, when my heroines choose their lovers, they need to feel some degree of trust, of emotional bonding. In those novels, my characters have usually made love for the first time somewhere in

125

the middle third of the book, but in a few of my books, lovemaking has occurred much sooner.

If your hero and heroine are going to make love very soon after first meeting, you'll need to create a situation where their motivation makes sense to you, to them, and to the reader. In a romance novel you want your reader to identify with your hero and heroine. Most romance readers are women. You want each of them to feel able to fantasize herself as the heroine, swept away by this hero.

If your heroine is promiscuous, your reader is unlikely to want to identify with her. But most readers are willing to enjoy a fantasy where the heroine is swept away, where she tosses caution to the winds and takes a lover — so long as the heroine's actions are believable and well-motivated. If your heroine makes love to the hero on first meeting, be sure your reader understands *why* she did it.

In stressful situations, people often behave in uncharacteristic ways. In writing about characters behaving uncharacteristically, focus on the mood, the sense of unreality that stress brings to your character.

Here are some situations where my heroines succumbed early to lovemaking.

- *Hidden Memories*. When Abby realizes that her husband Ben never loved her, she's completely disillusioned. Only moments later, their taxi is involved in a crash that results in his death. Abby wanders out of the hospital in shock, and hours later encounters Ryan, a stranger with a strong physical resemblance to Ben. To Ryan, just returned from the horrors of the war-torn Middle East, Abby seems like his fantasy woman. He invites her home. She goes with him, moving through the numbness of her shock and grief.

  She wanted to ask him to hold her, because she was ice and cold and lonely and frightened. He sat beside her, touching her face and looking into her eyes. "That's better," he whispered, and even without clear vision she saw too much in his eyes. His hand touched her cheek and she felt it. She knew that she must not feel. She must be only a ghost, slipping through a dream.

  Ben...

  She closed her eyes and reached for Ben's face. He touched her lips with his. Ben's kiss on her mouth.

- *One Secret Too Many.* The daughter of a minister and a pillar of virtue in her community, Alex has grown up knowing she must never do anything shocking. But for years she's been writing in secret, and now a publisher wants to publish her shocking mystery novel. When she sent the manuscript to the publisher, she was hoping for comments, encouragement. She never dreamed he'd offer to buy it. Alex knows she can't publish her book. While she's taking a solitary walk on the beach, immersed in the fantasies she knows she has to give up, she meets a man named Sam who somehow slips into her fantasy.

    They glided away from the night, deep into a secret darkness where the trees sheltered the world from them. Her lips parted and his head bent, touching her mouth with a soft promise.

    "Alex...Alexandra. You should have a knight on a white charger."

- *Storm.* Ever since her brother's death, Laurie has done everything she can to please her family, including becoming engaged to their vision of her ideal man. When she interviews Luke, a pilot taking part in the search for a missing float plane, she's haunted by the memory of her own guilt in the plane crash that killed her brother. Laurie persuades Luke to let her accompany him on the search. Hours later, Laurie and Luke land the seaplane on a remote island to seek shelter from bad weather. In the storm that follows, Laurie relives the old tragedy and, when her emotional storm is past, finds herself in Luke's arms.

    She watched the dark movement of a tree against the sky. She tried to think of tomorrow. When she tried to think of Ken, there was only a shadowy nothingness. Somewhere, a part of her knew that reality was tomorrow and Queen Charlotte and Ken...not Luke Lucas on a stormy, deserted North Pacific Island. But the weatherman had issued a storm warning, and he had been right. The storm was everywhere...outside her and within her. Tonight there was only one reality.

    "I cannot imagine tomorrow," she whispered.

c. Furthering the story objective

Your romance novel is a story in which the main characters struggle to overcome obstacles to romantic love and to achieve a happy ending. Your story objective is to portray hero and heroine battling

The first time hero and heroine make love may spark important changes in their relationship.

to overcome the obstacles to lifetime partnership. Anything that makes a happy ending more difficult belongs in your story, as does any action that brings lovers closer and any event which marks an important change in characters' feelings or behavior to each other.

The first time hero and heroine make love may mark important changes in their relationship. They have crossed a barrier, let down guards to intimacy. They may have shown each other a vulnerability that wasn't exposed before. In the aftermath, they may become closer, more trusting of each other, and begin to look at themselves as a couple. On the other hand, one or both lovers may experience panic after this intimacy.

A man may feel frightened at intimacy and feel the need to withdraw. A woman may crave closeness and reassurance. When he withdraws, she may feel he's rejecting her. Because men and women often react differently to increased intimacy, and because lovemaking changes relationships, lovemaking may often drive a wedge between lovers rather than bringing them closer.

If your characters' lovemaking complicates their relationship, or reveals hero and heroine to each other in new ways that increase their emotional intimacy, it's important to your story. If you're uncertain whether a love scene belongs in your story, try removing it. Make a fresh copy of your book on your computer and delete the love scene from the copy. If you can delete the scene without seriously affecting the plot, it doesn't belong in your novel. A love scene that belongs should have a measurable affect on the subsequent actions of both hero and heroine.

d. Your characters' feelings

Romance fiction is primarily women's fiction. An emotionally moving love scene speaks to women's natures, focusing on the feelings of the lovers, on the sensation of being swept away by passion and romance.

The secret to writing a good love scene is to remember that it is a love scene, not a sex scene. Your reader wants to feel the heroine's, and sometimes the hero's, emotions. She wants to feel the romantic sensation of being swept away by love as she touches her lover, of touching another human being's feelings more closely than she ever believed possible. She wants to feel the emotional love hero and heroine feel for each other that is expressed in the release of their sexual tension.

Reread your favorite romance novel. Stop when you get to the end of the first love scene. Read it again. Note the words and phrases that you respond to most strongly. Whether the scene describes physical details of lovemaking, or only the emotions that accompany it, note the words, phrases, and images that move you.

Making love is an important emotional milestone in the journey of two lovers. It can be described without being described at all, as in the case of Alex and Sam's consummation in my romance, *One Secret Too Many*.

> *He had said he would protect her, and despite her innocence she knew what he meant. A good thing, she thought wildly, because things were slipping away…and Alex was a reckless wench.*

Or it can be described with attention to the sensual details of lovemaking. In either case, the love scene will gain its power from its potent affect on the emotions and the lives of hero and heroine.

e. Once again, darling

You've written hero and heroine's first love scene, and the emotional effects it had on their relationship. Perhaps they've become regular lovers, continuing their sexual relationship while they struggle to overcome obstacles to a more permanent relationship. Should you let the reader see the next time hero and heroine make love?

Whether it's the first love scene or the fiftieth, the rule remains the same. Lovemaking belongs in your book only when it furthers the objective of the story.

f. Romance and safe sex

Your hero and heroine are falling in love. It's a romance, a fantasy. Is it necessary to mention condoms? Do you have to spoil the atmosphere by mentioning dangers such as AIDS and unwanted pregnancies?

Once a writer signs a contract with a publisher, she has no power to choose who reads the book. It belongs to anyone willing to pay the price in a bookstore, and anyone else the owner might lend it to. Romance readers range from teenage girls to women in their nineties. I don't believe it's okay to have irresponsible sex, and I wouldn't want to suggest to one of my teenage readers that it is. Consequently, most of my heroes and heroines give some thought to the issue of protection from disease and pregnancy.

But do remember that you're writing romance. It's not necessary to detail how a condom is used. It's often enough to mention that protection was used. Some writers have found romantic ways to use condoms in love scenes. Others have found a variety of creative ways in which to address the issue of safe sex without destroying the romance of a love scene.

Try finding your own.

16.

Suspense and story questions

A good story begins by stirring a question in the reader's mind: the *story question*. In a romance novel, the overriding story question is usually: Will heroine and hero overcome the obstacles to love and find their happy ending? If you've succeeded in making the reader ask this question, and if you've made the reader care about your characters, she will probably keep reading until the question is answered. In the course of finding the answer to that overriding question, many other questions will be asked — and answered.

Human beings are naturally curious creatures who feel a need to have their questions answered. Your readers will keep reading your books if they want answers to questions about your characters.

a. Rules of suspense

1. Don't answer the overriding story question until the end

In *The Moon Lady's Lover*, I began the book with Cynthia Dyson-Paige crossing North America by air, on her way to ask Jonathan Halley to loan her a great deal of money.

I knew my reader would suspect Jonathan is the hero, and would ask the question, "Will Cynthia and Jonathan have a happy ending?" Until page 189 when Jonathan and Cynthia overcome the last barrier to their happy ending, I was careful not to answer this question. I kept throwing obstacles in Jonathan and Cynthia's way — or to be more accurate, Jonathan and Cynthia created their own obstacles.

2. Don't answer an individual story question before creating a new one

Unanswered questions create suspense.

Suspense is created by unanswered questions. The greatest suspense is created by unanswered questions that threaten a character's health, safety, or happiness. Readers want the answers, but readers also want to be tormented, to have the answer withheld just long enough to heighten suspense.

By the time Cynthia meets Jonathan on page eight, I've tried to give the reader reason to add a number of questions to the happy-ever-after question: Why does Cynthia need money so desperately? Will Jonathan give Cynthia the money? If he does, what will he want in return? I've also tried to show Cynthia's emotional distress at meeting Jonathan again, to heighten the tension and suspense created by these questions.

Before I answer any of these questions, I invite the reader to ask another.

> *If anyone in her life could be called her enemy it was Jonathan Halley. And it was mutual because, when she stepped into that construction trailer and all the men turned to look at her, Jonathan was the one who didn't smile. The echo of relaxed camaraderie was still lurking among the blueprints but his black eyes turned cold when they saw her.*

What created this tension between Cynthia and Jonathan? Why haven't they spoken a friendly word to each other since Cynthia was a teenager?

As Jonathan and Cynthia talk money, I encourage yet another question.

> *"Why doesn't Allan approach me himself?"*
>
> *"I imagine he hates you. After what you did to him —"*
>
> *Jonathan twisted the glass in his hand. "What did I do to him?"*
>
> *"For heaven's sake, Jonathan! You know! You —"*
>
> *"Talk nicely when you want money," he suggested softly.*

What does Cynthia believe Jonathan did to Allan? Why doesn't Jonathan show any guilt?

By this time the reader has a whole host of questions. It's time to answer a couple of questions to make the reader believe more answers are coming.

Yes, Jonathan will loan the money, but in return he wants Cynthia to marry him. The reader has one question answered, only to be presented with a new batch. Why would Jonathan suggest such a crazy thing? Will Cynthia agree? Does Jonathan love Cynthia, or is he manipulating her for another reason? Does he want a relationship, or does he have ulterior motives in marrying her?

Questions provide motivation for readers to keep turning pages. If the story never provides answers, the reader becomes discouraged. If all the questions are answered too quickly after being posed, the reader becomes bored. If some questions are answered, and more presented, the reader feels suspense and a drive to keep reading until all the answers are discovered.

3. Let new questions continue to emerge

For the reader to believe in the eventual happy ending and to care about the characters, the characters must be fighting to achieve their own victory. As your story progresses, your characters must achieve both victories and setbacks.

Once Cynthia and Jonathan marry, Cynthia begins to believe Jonathan truly cares about her. But while they achieve temporary euphoria in lovemaking during their honeymoon, the reader knows the questions will come back to haunt hero and heroine. Why won't Jonathan answer Cynthia's questions about the past? What's the truth about the accident that crippled Allan, and why does it still overshadow the relationship between Cynthia and her husband?

Lovemaking is given tension by the reader's knowledge that the overriding story question hasn't yet been resolved: Will Cynthia and Jonathan overcome their problems to achieve true intimacy and a happy ending? How can they find a happy ending if Jonathan refuses to talk about the past?

> As your story progresses, your characters must achieve both victories and setbacks.

b. The beginning: an opening hook

In the bookstores, supermarkets, and drug stores, readers scan dozens of books to choose the one they want to read today. They look for a cover that appeals, for the name of an author they've read and enjoyed before, for a title that sounds interesting. They scan the paragraph on the back cover, wondering if this book will be a good read. They open the cover and flip to chapter 1 to read the first paragraph. If that first paragraph doesn't catch a reader's interest, she's unlikely to buy the book, and will probably never read it.

How can you interest your reader in just one paragraph? You need time to set up your characters, your story situation, and your conflict — all the things that make your story work.

You need time, but your reader won't give you the time you need unless you can assure her it will be worth it. There are thousands of other books she could be reading. Why should she assume yours is the best choice?

If you can hook your reader's curiosity with an unanswered question, she's likely to give you the time you need to explain who these people are and why she should care. But you don't have much time. To catch the reader, you need an opening hook in the first paragraph of your novel, preferably in the first sentence.

> **The first-paragraph hook can be a small mystery, but it should *never* be meaningless.**

The first-paragraph hook can be a small mystery, but it should never be meaningless. It should relate to your character and the story situation, and it should lead to other questions.

Because I didn't understand the importance of opening hooks when I wrote my first romance novel, I began *Pacific Disturbance* this way:

> *The spring winds had been blowing all day, whipping the waters of the harbor into ever-increasing turbulence.*

I went on to describe a windy day in Prince Rupert harbor. Reading *Pacific Disturbance* now, I think the stormy-day description was a poor beginning for a modern novel. A reader with a love of the ocean and windy days might enjoy reading it, but I've done nothing to stimulate curiosity about the rest of the book. By the end of page one, I doubt if the reader has thought of one question to ask.

I could have improved it by slipping in some action:

> *Max searched the shore as Wanderlust fought her way through the turbulent waters of the harbor. Was this the place?*

At least now the reader might wonder why Max is searching the shore.

Some years ago I became fascinated by the opening paragraphs of mystery writer Dick Francis, who has a wonderful talent for creating intense suspense in the first few words. I read book after book by Francis, absorbing the way he invariably hooked me in the very first paragraph. I began looking at the way other bestselling writers stirred my curiosity in the first few words.

From examining my own reactions as I read other writers' books, I learned that the curiosity stirred by the first few words of a book needn't be monumental. It can concern something quite trivial, as long as it relates to the larger story in a meaningful way and makes me wonder "what next?"

In *One Secret Too Many*, I began the first paragraph,

> *She was alone, looking out over glassy black water, streaks of colored light stretching from tall buildings on the shore of English Bay.*

I knew that if I began a book saying "she was alone," many readers would immediately wonder why. Because I also knew that if I didn't follow up in the next paragraph or two, my readers would forget the question, I intensified it in the next paragraph.

> *It was strange to her, this solitude. No one in the world knew where she was. No one would miss her if she stayed on the beach all night.*

I didn't explain why my heroine was alone. I knew better than to solve this small mystery before I'd created new mysteries. I left the question unanswered as I described my heroine and introduced her to the hero on the lonely beach.

When hero and heroine have known each other before, it's easy to stir questions in the reader by beginning with the reunion. I began *Hidden Memories* with the words, "It couldn't be him!" in a deliberate effort to stir questions in my readers: Who is he? Why is she so upset at the sight of him? Why so surprised at finding him here? By the time I answered these questions, I'd had time to tell the reader more about heroine and hero and to introduce new questions.

In *With Strings Attached*, hero and heroine had never met before the beginning of the book. To provide suspense in the first two paragraphs, I used a cat and an urgent journey.

> *"Happy birthday, Molly. The cabin's yours, but get out there right away. I've left Trouble with food for a day or two, that's all..."*
>
> *Pack up at a moment's notice? Drive three thousand miles in a tearing hurry to rescue a cat! No one but Saul would have the nerve to demand such a crazy favor. No one but Molly would be gullible enough to agree.*

While my reader is wondering who Saul is, and how he could abandon a cat, I have time to show you who Molly is, and to introduce her new neighbor, Patrick.

Look at the beginning of your story. If reading your first paragraph doesn't suggest any questions, try changing the words to create suspense and curiosity in your reader. If that doesn't work, try beginning the story at a different point.

c. *The middle: Problems and conflict, resolution hidden*

As your story progresses, the problems your characters face must form a logical progression, but at the same time the reader and the characters must remain uncertain of what will happen next. Ideally, new complications will strike the reader with a sense of *retrospective inevitability* — they aren't predictable, but once they occur they seem inevitable given what the reader already knows about the characters.

> **New complications should strike your reader with a sense of retrospective inevitability.**

If you begin your story with a clear idea in your mind of the nature of the conflict between hero and heroine, it will be easier to ensure that every problem they encounter leads them closer to wrestling with the real issue. Whatever that issue is, to maintain suspense in your novel, you must not finish resolving the core conflict until near the end of the book.

In *The Moon Lady's Lover*, I intended from the beginning that before Cynthia could find a happy ending with Jonathan, she must overcome her distrust and the fear that he would again reject her. Although she believed she could solve this problem by finding out what really happened between Jonathan, her brother, and her father in the past, I knew the issue was deeper. I knew Cynthia must overcome the scars of her battered-child past and learn to trust Jonathan's love without looking for evidence to disprove it.

I maintained suspense in the story by moving Cynthia through a series of problems, each of which brought with it a score of unanswered questions:

- Cynthia goes to ask Jonathan for money, believing he owes it to her brother Allan. The reader learns there's a past relationship between Cynthia and Jonathan, but the details are buried in the mystery of the night Allan was crippled in a car accident.

- Jonathan agrees to lend the money if Cynthia will marry him. Cynthia laughs this suggestion off, but can't think of any other way to avert bankruptcy. When she tells Allan she's asked Jonathan for money, he's mysteriously upset.

- Jonathan tempts Cynthia by offering to negotiate a marriage-for-money deal on whatever terms she wants.

- Cynthia's belief she can cope with the negotiated terms of her marriage is rocked when Jonathan tears up the contract and tells her she's free, saying he wants a real marriage. Indebted, her conscience won't let her walk away.

- Cynthia's growing desire for a real marriage with Jonathan wars with her memories of the way he once rejected her. On their honeymoon, he persuades her they must leave the past in the past.

- The euphoria of their relationship carries Cynthia back to her office after the honeymoon. When she sees a newspaper article revealing that Jonathan owned a significant block of her company's shares before the marriage, she's terrified she's been tricked again. She attacks him in a rage and subsequently refuses to see him except at public events.

d. The black moment: When all seems lost

The developing conflict between hero and heroine culminates in a black moment, a time when all seems lost. To be powerful, the black moment must come out of the personality and hang-ups of your characters, and it must be intimately related to the developing conflict issue of the book. The more powerful your black moment, the more satisfying will be the resolution that follows it.

> The black moment should come out of the personality and hang-ups of your characters.

In *The Moon Lady's Lover*, the black moment occurs when Jonathan tries to reconcile with Cynthia. When he explains that his reasons for buying her company's stock were not hostile, she believes him, but realizes she can't forget the past. She tells Jonathan she can never trust their relationship because she will always fear he'll leave her again. Cynthia and Jonathan have arrived at a point where resolution is impossible. Cynthia cannot forget the past, cannot trust Jonathan not to turn her away again, and as much as the reader can see he loves her, Jonathan will not talk about it.

If Cynthia can't let the past go, and Jonathan can't talk about it, their relationship is doomed. This is the black moment, when they turn away from each other.

e. The resolution: Something sacrificed to gain a happy ending

It is now, realizing they've lost each other, that both hero and heroine will realize how much they care about each other.

Every one of your readers has experienced loss. They've all loved and been hurt, wanted relationships that didn't work, been betrayed and abandoned. They've lost boyfriends, best friends, children, parents, grandparents, lovers, and partners. And every one of them has thought about how he or she might have done it differently.

When your characters experience a black moment where resolution seems impossible, each of your readers has personal experience of what it feels like to lose a relationship. Your readers understand the pain — the realization that what really matters is the relationship.

At this point, in the aftermath of the black moment, your characters have an opportunity to realize the relationship between them matters more than the convictions they held so rigidly. Jonathan has held stubbornly to his refusal to talk about the past. Cynthia has clutched her need for explanations before she can trust. Now, alone, both realize the relationship matters more.

Cynthia realizes she can't let Jonathan go. She goes to her brother Allan to demand an explanation of the past Jonathan won't talk about. When Allan won't talk either, she finally stops looking at the past and examines the reality of her present-day relationship with Jonathan. She finally sees that he loves her and knows she must let the past go.

I might have set the story up so that Jonathan explained the past to Cynthia earlier in the book, but Cynthia would not have faced her own doubts so clearly. I needed Cynthia to understand that she knew Jonathan better than anyone else on earth, that she knew the kind of man he was. I needed her to believe in his virtue because of what she knew about him, and to realize that whatever the hidden truth about that night when she was 16, Jonathan had behaved honorably and had always loved her. For the purposes of my story, it was important for Cynthia to wrestle with her doubts and overcome them without the aid of explanations that exonerated Jonathan.

The reader has a right to the answers, though, so once Cynthia made her decision to let go of the past, I had Allan tell her the truth.

I also needed to give the reader a good reason for Jonathan's refusal to talk about the past. I dealt with that in the moments after Jonathan and Cynthia reunited, at the end of the book.

When your characters achieve their happy ending, it's important that they sacrifice something to earn their happiness. Cynthia sacrificed her righteous insistence on knowing the truth about the past. Cynthia and Jonathan also sacrificed their protective covering, as every romantic hero and heroine must. To achieve a happy ending, lovers must always give up their need to protect themselves against abandonment. They must allow themselves to become vulnerable, to stand in front of each other without shields or armor. They must give up the illusion of safety that people create by shielding their emotions from others, must risk broken hearts and grief to gain the prize of true intimacy and life partnership.

It is only in the final scene of the romance novel, when hero and heroine make their sacrifice to emerge victorious over the conflicts that threaten their future, that the author should end the reader's suspense by answering the overriding story question: Can hero and heroine overcome their problems to find true intimacy and live happily ever after?

17.

Pacing and time

When I sent my fifth book to my editor, she told me the pacing was off. I hadn't a clue what she was talking about. I thought of horse races. I thought of books one to four, and wondered what I'd done differently in book five.

Pacing is about time, but in a novel, there are three different measures of time:

(a) *The writer's time,* or how long it took to write the book. For the writer, a six-page scene might feel endless if it took weeks to write.

(b) *The story time,* or time from the characters' viewpoint. In *The Touch of Love,* the story covered 105 days of my characters' lives.

(c) *The reader's time,* the three or four hours she spends reading the book, or the month she spends because she kept putting it down again.

a. Whose time?

In my novel, *The Touch of Love,* Scott Alexander is captain of an icebreaker in the arctic. He lives alone when he's not working. He's not a family man, and when his sister dies he's desperate to find a good home for her baby. Melody Connacher is a songwriter living alone on an isolated island. The baby's father is her twin brother.

A lot will happen before Scott and Melody achieve their happy ending. They must travel the emotional distance from solitude to partnership, and the 105 days from April 8 to July 22.

Pacing is about how I allocate 105 days of Scott and Melody's life into 55,000 words, the length of the book. However I divide those 105 days, it's essential to keep my reader's interest through every word. If I define the pace of a novel as the number of words or pages per unit of story time, the average pace in *The Touch of Love* would be 22 words an hour.

b. The pacing formula

At 22 words an hour, if I wrote an evenly paced book, eight hours of story-time sleep would get 176 words.

Here's the first night after Melody meets Scott:

> *She went into her music room and closed the door. She closed the shutters, too, and finally, in the quiet of the night, she was able to work.*
>
> *She woke early, before the alarm rang.*

I gave Melody's sleep a double space and no words. Those hours of sleep weren't important, so I didn't show them to the reader.

Wednesday night, two nights later, Melody isn't sleeping well. She wakes up twice. This night's sleep is important because it's the hero's fault she's not sleeping well, so I give Melody's time in bed a page and a half. Finally, she gets up and four pages later the first kiss occurs. Those four pages describe an important half hour, bringing Melody from her uncomfortable sleep into Scott's arms.

> *She stopped abruptly, but he was only half an arm's length away, between her and the door. She could see the bulge of his chest muscles, his heavy biceps pressing against his naked chest. She looked down, could not seem to stop herself, and his chest hair thickened as she followed it, then thinned as it trailed down to the waist of his jeans.*
>
> *He had not taken the time to put his belt on.*
>
> *He was watching her, seeing everything. The way his naked chest affected her, her own awareness of his eyes on her. Her body, breasts swelling in some mysterious woman's reaction to his man's chemistry. There were no words, but so much said. He was closer, and in a second his lips would take hers.*

That's just the introduction to the first kiss. Although the kiss took only a couple of minutes of Scott and Melody's life, I gave it 292 words. It was important.

If it's important, give details. If not, get it over quickly, making a narrative bridge to the next important event.

In an evenly paced book, a first kiss — that marvelous experience of nervousness and excitement — would get a third of a word.

The rule of thumb for pacing is simple: If it's important, give details. If not, get over it quickly, making a narrative bridge to the next important event.

c. Scenes and sequels

A novel is made up of scenes. After each scene comes a sequel which forms a bridge to the next scene. Scenes use up a lot of words because emotionally important things are happening. That first kiss was part of a scene, an intense emotional experience. In contrast, sequels cover a lot of character time with only a few words. They have low emotional value. The double space that represented Melody's uneventful sleep was part of a sequel.

Most novels are focused around a few important scenes. When reading scenes, the reader wants to see, touch, and breathe the viewpoint character's reality. In that first kiss scene, the reader needs to know all the little details that catch Melody's imagination. The pattern of Scott's muscles and the way the hair on his chest grows. The crazy thoughts going through Melody's head. The sensations on her skin.

> **After each scene comes a sequel which forms a bridge to the next scene.**

Emotionally loaded details speed the pacing and create emotional intensity. For Melody, time almost stops. For the reader, time flies and she reads the words faster.

> *He was watching her, seeing everything. The way his naked chest affected her, her own awareness of his eyes on her. Her body, breasts swelling in some mysterious woman's reaction to his man's chemistry. There were no words, but so much said...*

All these words and nothing has happened. No physical action, but if I did it right the reader is breathing faster, reading faster, and her fingers are tighter on the page. Fast pace means the reader feels she's moving fast, getting dizzy from the pace. To achieve a fast pace, the writer must use more words to describe less action, words designed to make the reader feel what the character feels.

Ideally your story will be composed of several fast-paced scenes with sequels between. The sequels give the reader time to get her breath, to calm down, to feel as if she's slowing down while you prepare her for the next scene. It's the reader's sensation of fast or slow motion that counts, not the days gone by in story time.

In *The Touch of Love*, after the first love scene between Melody and Scott, several days go by in less than a page. I create a slow pace by slipping into narrative mixed with introspection, telling about events rather than showing them. Because the reader feels story time going by without many sensations, the emotional pace is slow.

> *Melody wanted to meet Robin in Hawaii, but could not accept the idea of leaving Robbie behind with Mrs. Winston. The housekeeper had not been very much of a mother substitute for Melody and Robin. Maybe Robbie was too small to notice, but he had already lost his mother. He needed stability.*
>
> *But to tell Robin about Donna's death on the telephone.*

I go on to describe the days that follow, using about a page in total for this sequel, a bridge between the scene where Melody and Scott make love and the next significant event. I create a slow emotional pace by drawing back from my heroine's viewpoint.

In the kiss scene and the lovemaking scene, I showed the reader what Melody saw, felt, and touched. Now I back off, telling the reader that Melody wants to go to Hawaii without showing the details of the days when she makes that decision. I tell the reader, "the housekeeper hadn't been very much of a mother substitute," hinting at a sequence of events in Melody's childhood without letting the reader see those events.

This sequel passage is narrative. I'm stepping back to tell my reader what's happening, to distance her from the characters' emotions, give her a break between two emotional, significant scenes. I've changed my camera lens to wide angle, using one page to give the reader a glimpse of years of Melody's childhood, days of time where she doesn't go to Hawaii. Because the reader doesn't see the details, she feels the story has slowed down. This sequel between scenes gives the reader a brief break from the action, a breathing space.

d. The ebb and flow of pacing

As you reread your own scenes, pretend this is a book you've picked up at the grocery store.

1. Speeding the pace

If you find yourself wanting to skip over your own words, if they're not holding your attention as you read, speed up your pace by giving your important scenes more words. Show sounds, smells, sights, and sensations in your scenes. In the sequels between scenes, cut the words down, summarizing events by telling about them in fewer words.

Examine your scenes closely. Does each have an important effect on your characters? Does it either move your characters closer to the story objective, or oppose their reaching that objective? Examine each piece of information in a questionable scene. No matter how beautiful the images a passage evokes, if it isn't significant to the story objective, it doesn't belong in your novel. If a scene isn't significant to your story, to your characters, or to the conflict issue, shorten it to a sequel or get rid of it.

2. Slowing the pace

If your reader has no time to absorb the importance of scene one before you dump her into scene two, she'll be in sensory overload. Too many details will make the story lose its edge for the reader. If every part of *The Touch of Love* had the wealth of sensory detail I gave to Melody and Scott's first kiss, my reader would lose track of what she was reading because of too many details and not enough time to reflect on them.

To slow the pace and give your reader breathing space, summarize less important events in a narrative sequel, reducing your reader's connection to your viewpoint character's perceptive senses — telling about events briefly rather than showing sounds, smells, sights, and sensations.

e. Pacing is about feelings

Pacing is about feelings and sensations.

Pacing is about feelings and sensations. In a fast-paced scene, the reader feels the passage of each moment more strongly. She's pulled into the action with realistic details. She feels the character's intensity, eyes skimming the words rapidly. After the intensity of a fast-paced scene, the writer needs to slow the reader down by summarizing events into a narrative sequel. The reader's heartbeat slows, her eyes drift more slowly over the words. Because there's hardly any sensory information for the reader — no sights, no sounds, no smells or sensations — the reader feels slowed down.

In *The Touch of Love,* I used a slow pace to form a sequel just before a scene with high emotional content.

> *She stared through the window at the smooth, shining*
> *water of the little bay, the narrow gorge that opened out*
> *to the ocean.*

In this short bit I've deliberately used narrative to slow down emotionally and give the reader time to prepare for what's coming. Then, moving into the scene, I sped up the pace by going deeper, giving emotionally important detail.

> *She said, "I thought you should know, that you had a right*
> *to know… I'm pregnant."*
>
> *She turned and he was staring at her. She wasn't sure*
> *what it was in his eyes. He blinked and she thought maybe*
> *it was shock. She had wanted it to be joy, but she should*
> *have known to keep the fairy tales in her music room.*
>
> *He said slowly, "Say that again."*

All those words, and a half page more, for a few seconds of story time. Why? Because this passage has high emotional content. Hopefully my reader's eyes are racing, she's feeling the fast emotional pace. Intense emotions are tangled in Melody's words and sensations. It's the emotional intensity that creates the feeling of fast pace.

In moments of high emotional content, time should disappear for the reader even though it may take longer to read the words than the actions took for the character.

> *She clasped her hands together behind her back, licked her*
> *lips and whispered, "Do you love me?"*
>
> *His jaw flexed. Something in his eyes flared briefly and*
> *was gone. She felt tightness in her throat and swallowed.*

It probably takes longer to read the above words than it took for Melody to ask "Do you love me?" and Scott's jaw to spasm. Because it's important, the reader gets all the details, all the emotional content.

f. The pacing rule

The parts of your story that have high emotional impact should use more words per unit of character time. If hero and heroine are having an emotionally difficult conversation, you might use ten pages to show your reader this scene. Afterward, the heroine might spend a whole day on a shopping spree. The fact that the fight with the hero caused her to max out her credit cards is significant, but the shopping events aren't, so you'd probably deal with the shopping spree in a couple of paragraphs.

Fast pace is created by making the reader feel intense emotions.

Pacing is about the reader's feeling of moving quickly. Fast pace means the reader reads the words faster, and loses track of time on her clock. If you're writing an important event or behavior, give details. If it's a secondary or unimportant event, pass over it quickly with a narrative bridge to the next important thing.

If you want to study pacing further, read *Writing Novels that Sell* by Jack M. Bickham. In chapter 9 of his book, Bickham illustrates the effect of different writing techniques — narration, dramatic action, dialogue, description, and exposition — of pacing.

Pacing Guidelines

Pacing — whose time?

Story time (105 days)

Writer time (500 hours)

Reader time (3 hours)

The pacing rule: If it's an important event or behavior, give details. If it's unimportant, pass over it quickly with a narrative bridge to the next important thing.

- Fast pace is created by making the reader feel intense emotions.

- Fast pace means fast emotional pace for the reader.

- Fast pace means the reader reads the words faster, and loses track of time.

A novel = scenes + sequels

- A sequel = a bridge between scenes.

- Scenes are important and should be emotionally fast-paced.

- Sequels (bridges) are secondary and should be emotionally slower-paced.

Pacing is connected to everything in your story

- As pacing changes, viewpoint changes: the fast pace is deeper in character viewpoint, the slow is shallower.

- As you shift from scene to sequel, pacing changes. The scene feels close and fast, the sequel or bridge feels slow and farther away.

- Pacing changes as significance changes. Significant events get more words and the reader feels a fast pace. Secondary events are ignored or dealt with in a few words, reader feels a slower pace.

18.

Viewpoint and emotional intensity

a. Whose eyes?

Whose eyes will your reader use to see your romance story? Will it be the hero's eyes? The heroine's? What viewpoint will you use to tell your story?

1. First person viewpoint

In first person viewpoint, the story is told as if the narrator were the writer: "I remember when I first met Jake. It was a dark and stormy day. He looked angry as he rode over the hill." The viewpoint character narrates the story in first person, as she might verbally or in a journal. The author is limited to the events this character can perceive, and cannot tell the reader the thoughts of other people in the story unless the narrator comes to know them. First person viewpoint is often used in mystery stories, particularly detective mysteries. It's less common in romances, and is almost never seen in category romances.

2. Third person viewpoint

In third person viewpoint, the story is told through the eyes of a third person who observes from *inside* the viewpoint character's mind: "She remembered the day she first met Jake. It was a dark and stormy day. He looked angry as he rode over the hill." Third person frees the writer to chose a different viewpoint character for different parts of the book. This freedom allows a romance novelist to heighten tension by showing the heroine's internal conflict, then shifting to the hero to show his internal conflict.

When more than one character's point of view is used in a novel, it is termed *third person multiple viewpoint*. In short contemporary romances, it's common to see both the hero and heroine's viewpoint in third person. In longer romances, viewpoints of other characters are sometimes included. Third person multiple viewpoint is the most common viewpoint used for romance novels today, with the viewpoint generally restricted to hero and heroine.

3. Omnipotent viewpoint

In omnipotent viewpoint, the story is told through God's eyes, with the reader seeing into everyone's thought processes. "She remembered the day she first met Jake. It was a dark and stormy day. He was angry as he came over the hill, because he'd just fought with Meg." The reader sees everyone's thoughts and feelings, as if she were looking with some magical "X-ray" vision that sees all, knows all.

Omnipotent viewpoint is seldom used in modern fiction and should not be used in romance, because it distances the reader from the characters.

4. Author intrusion

Sometimes an author slips personal comments into a scene. "What Annie didn't know was that at that very moment, Harry was sneaking into the Shady Motel with her sister Joan." Author intrusion reminds the reader that she's reading a story, jolting her out of the fictional world. To keep your reader involved in your fictional world, you should avoid author intrusion.

5. Mixed viewpoints

Some writers mix first and third person, using first for one character and third for all others. This technique is often used in stories where journals or diaries make up part of the story; the journal is presented in first person as written, and the other characters appear in third person. Katherine Neville uses mixed first and third person in a different way in her mainstream romantic thrillers. In *The Eight* and *A Calculated Risk,* Neville uses first person for her present-day heroine, and third for historical characters, making it easy for the reader to separate the modern-day story from the related historical story.

b. Guidelines for viewpoint

1. Limit your viewpoint characters and shifts

Writing romantic fiction, you'll probably use third person viewpoint. At any point in your story, the character through whom the reader sees the story world is the *viewpoint* or *point-of-view* character. You want your reader to feel this character's emotions deeply. To achieve this, limit your point-of-view characters to those people who are most important to the story. If you write paragraphs and scenes from minor character viewpoints, the reader may feel distanced from the primary characters you most want her to care about.

I recommend you limit your viewpoint characters to hero and heroine at first. In a long romance, once you're comfortable with changing viewpoints, you can expand to include one or two other characters important to the story.

2. Limit your writing to what your viewpoint character can sense

Limit the information you give the reader to what your point-of-view character can see, hear, touch, taste, feel, and think. Otherwise the reader will feel confused and disconnected from the character.

Always limit your writing to what your viewpoint character can sense.

3. Avoid head-hopping

If you frequently hop back and forth from one character's thoughts to another's, the reader may lose her sense of involvement with your story. You want your reader to feel she's inside the mind of the viewpoint character, experiencing what that character experiences. Every viewpoint character should experience doubt about what other characters are thinking. Your heroine does not know the hero's thoughts, she can only guess. If you shift point of view too often, letting the reader in on everyone's thoughts as a scene progresses, the reader will tend to forget that these characters don't know each other's thoughts.

Let the reader feel the natural suspense and difficulty as your characters guess at each other's thoughts and motives.

4. Give clear signals when you change point of view

When you change from one viewpoint character to another, be sure the reader knows immediately that you've changed, otherwise she'll feel disoriented. You can use the following techniques to signal point-of-view changes to your reader.

- Give the reader a physical clue that you have changed viewpoint by changing at a chapter break, or showing a break in the text with an extra double space between paragraphs, or an extra double space and a line of three asterisks.

- In the first sentence with the new viewpoint character, give a clear clue by showing the reader something that can be seen only from the new viewpoint and naming the viewpoint character.

In *The Moon Lady's Lover*, I ended chapter 9 in Jonathan's viewpoint, then began chapter 10 in Cynthia's. In addition to a chapter break, I signaled Cynthia's viewpoint to the reader in the first two sentences of the new chapter.

End of chapter 9:

> *"Don't leave," he said, but she was running from him.*
>
> *He watched her go through the door and the night went darker.*

Beginning of chapter 10:

> *All her dreams had turned to nightmares. Cynthia stood in Jonathan's garden staring at the city lights and she didn't know where to go or what she could do now.*

Whether or not you have changed viewpoints, you should always give a clear signal of the viewpoint character in the first paragraph of any new chapter or section.

5. Be careful of mirrors and physical inventories

It can be challenging for a writer to find a way to tell the reader what a character looks like while in that character's viewpoint. Some writers have resorted to having the character look in a mirror and catalogue her assets: "She stared at herself in the mirror. Long blonde hair, curling slightly. Pale blue eyes. Narrow chin. Small nose. Full lips."

Because we seldom study ourselves in a mirror in this way, the reader seldom feels she's sharing this character's thoughts. The same is true of the self-inventory in which a character mentally catalogues his or her own appearance. Since an objective cataloguing of physical appearance isn't something we normally do, it strikes a false note to the reader.

If you use a mirror to reflect details of your character's appearance, or a self-inventory, restrict the character's thoughts to realistic ones. A woman dressing for a date will probably examine herself in a mirror, but be sure your character's thoughts are natural. Focus on the emotion the character is feeling, not the physical details, as in this passage from *From Nothing Less Than Love*:

> *She swallowed and stared at herself in the mirror. Her hair was still down, unruly waves reaching past her shoulders. Normally she had it done every morning by the girl from the hair salon on the main floor, twisted back in a knot that was both businesslike and elegant. She couldn't possibly manage to duplicate that style by herself, but she had to do something. She didn't want to go out to Alex with her hair curling everywhere in wild abandonment.*
>
> *She grabbed a brush and the pins and struggled with it until it was anchored and contained. She reached up both hands to twist in a stray strand and the sweater pulled against her, forming soft wool to the curves of her breasts. She dropped her arms abruptly and fought the surge of trembling that swept over her.*
>
> *She was not going to think that kind of thought!*

You don't need to tell the reader every physical detail about your character.

Remember, you don't need to tell the reader every physical detail about your character. In the above scene I showed a woman with wild hair she customarily pins up into a disciplined roll. I told the reader she's wearing a sweater she wishes would hide her feminine curves. This tells as much about her character as it does about her body. The reader knows this heroine is nervous and uncomfortably aware of her femininity. Imagination will fill in the other details: lips, eyes, facial shape.

6. Through other eyes

Writers often use viewpoint characters to tell the reader about other characters.

When you show one character's observations of another, remember to be consistent with the character doing the observing. If your hero, Jake, is a construction worker who grew up on the streets of Chicago, he's unlikely to look at the heroine and think, "She was wearing an aquamarine silk cocktail dress by de Lornier, with matching satin high heels." He's more likely to think, "She opened the door wearing a blue-green thing that swirled around her legs and had him clenching his fists, imagining her eyes would change color if he touched the soft white flesh exposed by her low neckline."

151

7. Don't get between your character and the reader

You know things about your character that the reader needs to know. One way to get the information across is to tell the reader directly.

> *Alice had always wanted to be a singer when she grew up. Her fifth grade teacher encouraged her ambitions, and at the age of 13 Alice performed solo in the church choir. Singing was her life: music lessons, theory. There was no time for boys and falling in love...*

There's a hint of author intrusion here. The writer is telling the reader about Alice, not showing her. To test for author intrusion, try rewording a passage in the first person to see if it sounds natural and in character.

> *I always wanted to be a singer when I grew up. My fifth grade teacher encouraged my ambitions, and at the age of 13 I performed solo in the church choir. Singing was my life: music lessons, theory. There was no time for boys and falling in love...*

In first person, the passage sounds stilted and unnatural. To keep your reader involved, you must help her forget this is a story. Sneak the background information into a scene naturally at a point where Alice has reason to reflect on her life dream of singing. The result will be more dynamic, and the reader will feel more involved with Alice.

> *"How about dinner" he asked. "Tonight?"*
>
> *Alice almost said yes, but over dinner he'd expect conversation. What did a woman talk about on a date? She'd never had a chance to practice — music lessons, voice coaching, solo performances in the school choir. No time for boys...for men. Until now, it hadn't mattered. Singing had been her life.*

Use your character's thoughts, words, and body language to reveal character history, goals, and hang-ups.

c. When to change viewpoint characters

If you finish chapter 5 in your heroine's point of view, how do you decide whether to start chapter 6 in her viewpoint, or the hero's?

1. Choose the viewpoint character who has most at stake

Each scene, or portion of a scene, should be written from the viewpoint of a character who has a high stake in the events of that scene.

For each scene, choose the viewpoint character who has most at stake.

For the reader to care what happens, she must feel that the scene is important. For the scene to seem important, it must be viewed through the eyes of someone to whom the events matter. Does your hero or heroine have a greater emotional investment in the upcoming scene? The answer may tell you who should be the point of view character.

Think of yourself as the director in a film with several cameras. If you're having trouble writing a scene, or portion of a scene, it may be time to change cameras for the next scene. Try shifting into another character's viewpoint and see if it works better.

2. Change viewpoint when necessary to explain motivation

Sometimes a character will do something that makes sense only if the reader can see inside that character's mind. When this happens, your decision of viewpoint character will depend on whether you want the reader to understand the motivation. If the hero says something that shocks the heroine, you may want the reader to remain in the dark about his motives until later in the story. To accomplish that, write the scene from the heroine's viewpoint and limit the reader's knowledge of the hero's motivation to what the heroine already knows.

On the other hand, you may feel the reader needs a better understanding of the hero. Writing *The Moon Lady's Lover*, I wrote chapter 1 from Cynthia's point of view to let the reader see both her desperation for the money she was asking to borrow and her belief Jonathan would lend it to her because of a feeling of responsibility for Cynthia's brother.

In chapter 2, Jonathan was going to agree to loan the money on condition she marry him. As they hadn't spoken a civil word to each other in years, I knew Jonathan's proposal would seem outrageous. I needed the reader to understand Jonathan had good reason for his action, so I began chapter 2 in Jonathan's viewpoint.

> *Jonathan Halley had always been a gambling man — not irrational wagers, but calculated acts of risk. He knew that there was sacrifice and benefit in every deal. He always tried to weigh the two and come out ahead.*
>
> *In the last few years he'd made deals that had made him millions. Once, when he was a kid of nineteen, he'd made a deal that had lost him Cynthia Dyson-Paige. He'd made the bargain and he'd kept his promise, but he didn't like it. And now Cynthia had come to him and the irony was that she wanted to bail her brother out of trouble.*

VIEWPOINT AND EMOTIONAL INTENSITY

In these two paragraphs, without giving details, I've established four important things: Jonathan is a man to take a gamble. He once considered the heroine his. Sometime in the past he made a promise that cost him Cynthia, a promise he didn't like but wouldn't break. And finally, all this has something to do with Cynthia's brother.

A few paragraphs later Jonathan says:

> *"I'll cover the note, but there is a condition, I want you to marry me, moon lady."*
>
> *He saw her hand clench. Her fingers were white but color crawled into her face from her throat.*
>
> *"You're crazy," she said.*

Because I wrote the scene from Jonathan's point of view, the reader knows Jonathan isn't crazy, he's taking a gamble, hoping to win back what he lost years ago.

3. Skip non-essential scenes

Don't hesitate to skip over events that the reader doesn't need to see directly.

If your only reason for writing a scene is to convey information to the reader, and neither primary character will be deeply affected by the events, consider skipping the scene and filtering the missing information into the next one.

In *The Moon Lady's Lover*, Cynthia agrees to try negotiating a marriage-for-money deal with Jonathan at the end of chapter 2. Most of the details of their negotiations aren't important to my story, only the results.

I ended chapter 2 in Cynthia's point of view:

> *"We're talking about it. That's all." She shivered. "I warn you, I drive a hard bargain."*
>
> *"So do I," he said with a grin. "But I do intend to make certain we don't regret it."*

I opened chapter 3 after the deal had been agreed:

> *They signed the contract in Warren Liturson's office twenty stories above the ground in Vancouver's financial district.*

I wrote both sections from Cynthia's point of view because she was the one in a state of emotional confusion. I wanted the reader to feel her confusion and indecision. Jonathan was clear in his motives at this point, he wasn't experiencing internal conflict, and the reader already knew his motives.

d. Viewpoint and the writer's camera

If you remain true to your character's viewpoint, you'll only allow your reader to see, hear, and feel what the character senses. But although you're limited by the boundaries of your point-of-view character's consciousness, you're free to vary the depth of that viewpoint.

The rule for viewpoint depth is simple: the more impact the event has on the viewpoint character, the deeper the writer should be in viewpoint.

Think of yourself as a camera operator capturing story action on film. When you want your reader to feel intensely connected with the action, you zoom in for a close-up. The reader falls deep into your character's viewpoint, seeing through her eyes, feeling through her fingers. The reader reads faster, feels more, and thinks less.

If you want your reader to catch her breath as she prepares for the next scene, change to your wide angle camera lens. The details aren't so clear now. There's more in the picture, more events captured in fewer words, the viewpoint is shallower. At the extreme, you may actually slip out of viewpoint and briefly watch your character instead of looking through her eyes.

Showing speeds the pace and involves the reader. In your scenes, where events important to your characters and your story are played out, show your reader what's happening in eyewitness fashion. When a passage has deep emotional significance, move deeper into character viewpoint, showing your reader a close-up view of your character's sensory experiences. When it has less significance, draw back slightly, using your words in the same way a photographer uses wide-angle and close-up lenses.

Telling slows the pace and distances the reader, who needs an occasional brief break from the intensity of your story. "Telling" passages should be brief and generally confined to the short sequels between your scenes.

> *Showing* speeds pace and involves the reader.
>
> *Telling* slows pace and distances the reader.

e. Viewpoint and pacing

Pacing a book involves finding the balance between showing and telling, between emotional intensity and distance, between slow and fast. It means giving a reader enough time to absorb what's happening, but not enough to turn away from the story events.

To get a feel for the effect viewpoint has on pacing, select a page of your book and rewrite it, first moving deep into your character's viewpoint, restricting your reader to the immediate input of your character's senses. In this deep viewpoint connection, don't allow your character to evaluate what she's sensing. Perception is instant-to-instant, without time to reflect. This deep viewpoint is appropriate for portions of scenes where your character is so overwhelmed by the moment that there is no time or capacity for evaluating the experience. Because the character is unable to reflect, the deep viewpoint connection creates a timeless feeling suitable for love scenes and moments of crisis where time seems suspended. For the reader, this deep viewpoint experience of the character's sensory inputs creates the sensation of overwhelmingly intense experience.

Next, rewrite the page from a slightly shallower viewpoint. Make your character, and the reader, aware of what's happening. Your prose becomes a mixture of your character's observations and thoughts about those observations. Your heroine may realize she forgot to take the garbage out while she's rushing to meet the hero. This everyday-eyewitness level of viewpoint gives the reader the feeling of sharing the character's experience and thoughts. The character and the reader both have an awareness of the passage of time. Variations of this level of viewpoint are what you'll use for the majority of your scenes.

Now, rewrite the events a third time, summarizing the entire passage into one sentence. To do this, you'll need to draw back to a very shallow viewpoint, telling the reader about the character rather than showing her.

As you take your new awareness of telling, showing, viewpoint, and pacing back to your romance novel, remember that the depth of your connection to the events of the story and the number of words you give each event must be in proportion to the importance of the events to the story and the characters.

f. Emotional intensity

When a book has emotional intensity, the reader feels the characters' emotions, both the suffering and the joy. This happens when the writer succeeds in writing deep in character viewpoint while the character is feeling deep emotions. For emotional intensity to be present in your novel, the characters themselves must have depth

Grace Green on...Developing Emotional Intensity

Editors have told you your work lacks emotional punch. You're trying to fix the problem...but are you on the right track? Find out by checking (a) or (b) below:

You've come up with an idea for a new book. You run with it because:

> *(a) the idea excites you*

> *(b) the idea is trendy*

After you've created your hero and heroine, you:

> *(a) spend time getting to know them before you start writing*

> *(b) plunge ahead because you've worked out this terrific plot*

When your hero and heroine are together and you're in your heroine's point of view, you:

> *(a) see only the hero because for the moment you "are" the heroine*

> *(b) see both characters clearly*

When you're writing from your hero's/heroine's point of view, you:

> *(a) bring him/her to life by using the five senses*

> *(b) walk him/her through the scene like a robot*

When your hero and heroine are conversing you make sure that:

> *(a) their thoughts/feelings are often in direct conflict with their dialogue*

> *(b) their thoughts/feelings are always in perfect harmony with their dialogue*

You choose your settings carefully and use them to:

> *(a) highlight the emotional state of your characters*

> *(b) showcase your brilliant descriptive skills*

You complete your first three chapters but your work seems wooden, so you:

> *(a) analyze favorite romances that have touched you deeply, and learn from them*

> *(b) concentrate even harder on telling the reader how your characters feel*

If you answered (a) each time, congratulations — you're on "the write track"!

and intensity. They must be well-developed whole people who care deeply about life and who feel things deeply.

The most important factor in creating emotional intensity is the author's willingness to delve into her own strong emotions. To write about a character's emotions, you must feel those emotions. If your character receives a painful rejection, remember a time when you were rejected. Let yourself feel that pain again. Is this how your character feels? What thoughts go with the feeling? Write about it. Reliving your own strong emotions can be difficult, but it's an important part of developing power in your writing.

19.

Telling, showing, and transitions

a. Telling versus showing

Molly was excited when her father told her he'd given her the cabin, but upset when he said she'd better hurry out there because he'd left the cat without much food.

In the above sentence from *With Strings Attached*, I've told you about a conversation between Molly and her father. I've told you she's upset and excited as a result of that conversation. When a writer tells her readers what happened and how the characters are feeling, the reader is cheated of the chance to see for herself what happened.

For the reader, a novel is a journey into fantasy, a love story she can imagine with all her senses. In this journey, the reader is an active participant. She creates pictures based on the writer's words. She draws conclusions about the characters' moods, emotions, and actions based on the pictures.

If the writer says, "Molly was excited," the reader wrestles with the word "excited." The above passage invites the reader to analyze the words "excited" and "upset," but gives no clues to stimulate visual images. The words that label emotions — sad, happy, excited, upset, jealous — never create a graphic picture of the emotion itself. By labeling an emotion, you drain away its power.

We've all been told since infancy not to believe what we don't see for ourselves. On some level, if I tell my reader Molly is excited, she

> **By labeling an emotion, you drain away its power.**

Telling versus Showing

Look at the following tell/show pairs and notice your response to the words. Which evokes the most graphic mental picture in your mind? Which invites more curiosity and questions into your mind? Which feels more exciting?

Tell: He kissed her softly. She trembled and felt breathless.

Show: The softest touch of hard, full lips against hers. She shivered and the touch returned, brushing, caressing, light, not demanding. She tried to breathe and she could not. She tried to step back, but he had her trapped with only those teasing lips. (from *The Touch of Love*)

Tell: Carrie was panic-stricken when she woke up in bed with Charles.

Show: Carrie lay very still. Around her, silently, the night shattered. Panic spun through her darkness. Silence here, but in the dream…

Soft, slow breath against her shoulder. And sensations. An echo of the dream, that warm heaviness on her hip. Deep inside her own sleep-drugged body she felt the slow shadow of heat from the place she had been. A man. Breathing. Holding her close. What had she done? (from *After All This Time*)

won't believe it. She doesn't see Molly being excited, doesn't *feel* sympathetic excitement.

If I *show* the reader Molly's thoughts, the passage comes alive.

> *"Happy Birthday, Molly. The cabin's yours, but get out there right away. I've left Trouble with food for a day or two, that's all…"*
>
> *Pack up at a moment's notice? Drive three thousand miles in a tearing hurry to rescue a cat! No one but Saul would have the nerve to demand such a crazy favor. No one but Molly would be gullible enough to agree.*

In this passage, I didn't give many details of Molly's conversation with her father. The reader doesn't know where Molly was when this conversation took place, what she was wearing, if she was standing or sitting, alone with Saul or at a party. Each reader will form her own picture of Molly's surroundings.

By showing a scrap of Molly's conversation with her father, and her tangled, frustrated thoughts as a result, I've left the reader free to decide for herself whether Molly is excited, upset, frustrated, or angry. Different readers might label Molly's emotions differently, but each reader will feel she's sharing Molly's feelings to some degree.

You want your readers to feel the intensity your characters' experience. To achieve this and give your writing intensity, show your characters' emotions and experiences. Showing strengthens the reader's fantasy and creates reader involvement.

When you've shown the reader an event or emotion, it's tempting to also label what you've just shown.

> *Jane's heart was pounding so hard she couldn't hear what he was saying. She clenched her hands into fists, felt her nails bite into her palms and wondered if there would be blood, wondered if he'd follow her if she ran out through that door. Jane was extremely upset.*

When you show the reader your characters' sensations and emotions, you are evoking the reader's own imagination, drawing on the creative, feeling part of the brain. After you've succeeded in getting the reader to move into fantasy and feel what your character is feeling, the last thing you want is to insert words that will move the reader back into logical, non-imaginative thought.

By labeling the emotions and events you've just shown the reader, you inevitably pull the reader out of her fantasy and into logical thought. The reader ends up comparing her experience of Jane's emotion with the label "Jane was upset" to decide whether she agrees. If the reader doesn't agree with the label, you've lost credibility. Worse, the reader has dropped out of your fantasy world to evaluate "Jane was upset."

When you finish writing your book, search for places where you've *shown* the reader, then followed the visual image by *telling* what you just showed. Take out the repetitious telling words.

b. How to show

To show the reader what's happening in a scene, focus your attention on your viewpoint character's perceptive senses. By giving your reader the sensory cues of eyes, ears, nose, mouth, and skin, you evoke graphic, realistic images and draw your reader into the story.

Showing words and phrases describe physical sensations experienced by the viewpoint character — touch, heartbeat, sounds, or the lack of them. By describing sensory input, you evoke corresponding emotions in your reader.

c. A place for telling

Showing evokes more powerful responses in the reader than telling, but you'll overwhelm the reader if you show her everything in your story. She needs to feel the important events and emotions in your book: the first kiss, the emotional turmoil of leaving a lover, the rising conflict between lovers. On the other hand, although the reader may need to know the heroine drove downtown, if the only purpose of the drive is to get your heroine from scene A to scene B, you're best to say, "She drove downtown," telling the reader in three words instead of taking two pages to show her.

If you kept up the intensity of a deeply emotional *telling* scene from the beginning of your book to its end, your reader would become exhausted. So would your characters. Both readers and characters need breathing spaces between scenes, time to shift to the next scene, to reflect on what went before and anticipate what is to come. These sequels or narrative bridges are generally much shorter than the scenes, and it's appropriate for them to contain more telling and less showing than scenes.

Showing always requires more words to communicate with the reader, but the images communicated are more graphic. Telling

Tell: Julie felt sick at the depth of her jealousy of David's dead wife.

Show: "If you touch me, take me, into that room, that bed, I'll know it's really her you want, that I'm only — you're...wishing I were her..."

She swallowed, hearing the echo of her own words. "I don't believe I said that," she whispered, "But it's true. That's how I feel." (from *When Love Returns*)

evokes less emotional response, uses fewer words, and allows writer and reader to span a large piece of time or experience in a few words.

The variation of telling and showing in your novel contributes to the pacing in your story.

d. Getting from here to there

When I first began writing fiction novels, like most writers I struggled with how to move my characters through time and space — from one scene to another, from one location to another, from one time to another.

I found myself listening to the words of songs in the music I played while I worked. In songs, the transitions aren't always logical. I realized that the important thing in transitions is to avoid confusion. I began using a variety of transitions, depending on the circumstances.

1. The break transition

The break is the simplest transition of all, similar to the changing of scenes in a play. In *Strangers by Day*, I ended chapter 4 with the heroine in the aftermath of being kissed by the hero. I began chapter 5 with the opening, "Faith made pastries in the kitchen...," shifting in time from darkness to the next day, and in space from Faith's bedroom to the kitchen downstairs.

If you shift time and place at the end of one chapter, check the chapter before and after. You don't want to use every chapter break to change scenes. Sometimes, the new chapter should continue the scene from the previous chapter, or your novel will become predictable and less exciting to the reader.

> **Readers will always be prepared for you to shift time, place, or viewpoint character at the end of a chapter.**

Readers will always be prepared for you to shift time, place, or viewpoint character at the end of a chapter. Therefore, it's important to begin each new chapter with an immediate signal of time, place, and viewpoint character.

Within a chapter, you can break between paragraphs to signal a transition from one time, place, or viewpoint character to another. Some writers show this sort of break with a double space and a centered line of one or more asterisks. Others simply use a double space. Whatever format you use, be consistent in your manuscript, and realize that your publisher will probably substitute the break style that is in common use in that publishing house.

In chapter 5 of *Strangers by Day,* Faith put her pastries in the oven, then went for a swim. On her way to the water she had a disturbing encounter with Max. At the end of this scene, I used a double space to leap both time and space.

> *Then she dropped the towel on the big rock at the water's edge, and something made her turn to face him.*
>
> *He was gone.*

> *The pastries were burned.*
>
> *Faith took the baking sheet out of the oven, cursing softly so that the words were indistinct.*

Like the chapter break transition, the double space transition can also be used to signal a change in viewpoint character.

2. The word picture transition

You can jump over time and space with a word picture. The following passage begins with the hero in the heroine's office on Monday morning:

> *"All right," Betty agreed. "Wednesday. I'll meet you at Alice's Restaurant."*
>
> *When Betty got to Alice's on Wednesday, he hadn't arrived yet. She sat at the table by the window, telling herself she didn't care if he stood her up.*

When Betty says "Wednesday" and "Alice's," the reader forms a mental picture of Betty at Alice's restaurant. If you shift immediately to Wednesday at Alice's, the reader will be waiting for you. To the reader, this transition will seem so smooth it may be invisible.

3. The concept transition

The word picture transition takes advantage of a word picture that's already been introduced to the reader and uses it to shift time and place to the location of the word picture. The concept transition uses a concept that's already been introduced to the reader as a bridge to the next scene. This transition, and the word picture transition, can be used alone or with a section or chapter break to give the reader a smooth flow of images from one scene to the next.

In chapter 2 of *The Moon Lady's Lover,* Jonathan suggests Cynthia might find marriage to him more attractive if they negotiate a marriage contract on her terms. Having introduced the idea of a marriage contract, I used the concept as a bridge to the next chapter, beginning chapter 3:

> You can jump over time and space with a word picture.

They signed the contract in Warren Liturson's office twenty stories above the ground in Vancouver's financial district.

By tying chapter 3 to the end of chapter 2 using the concept of a marriage contract, I was able to jump over the details of the negotiations between Jonathan and Cynthia and the trip from Parkland to Vancouver without mentioning them. The reader, focused on the theme of the marriage contract, should make the transition comfortably and arrive at Warren Liturson's office clinging to the common thread between the two scenes — the marriage contract.

4. The narrative bridge

In the above examples, the action moves from one scene to another with little time and no words between, and the reader follows without thinking about the time that separates them.

In your story, there will be places where you want the reader to be aware of time passing, and other places where you want to give transitory information before your reader arrives at the next scene. You can achieve both by drawing back from character viewpoint and using words like a wide angle camera, showing big hunks of time and geographical leaps in a few words or sentences.

In these narrative bridges you are telling your reader time is passing, not showing the reader in the sensory manner you portrayed the action of a scene. You'll want to create a feeling for the transition, to focus on an atmosphere and mood to suit your story and your viewpoint character. As you write your narrative bridge, remember what you want your reader to learn from it.

In chapter 5 of *The Moon Lady's Lover*, Jonathan and Cynthia arrive at a Mexican hotel for their honeymoon. I didn't want to describe their arrival and the first day in detail, so I used narrative to impart the atmosphere of the hotel and the fact that time is passing.

The beach at Cabo San Lucas was only a breath away from their suite. Both bedrooms and the sitting-room opened on to a tiled patio. Cynthia could step outside her bedroom and lean against the marble balustrade of the patio, staring at the ocean....

From this opening I went on to touch on the details of their arrival, using a few paragraphs to give the flavor of their first hours in that Mexican hotel and their tense interaction at the beginning of their separate-bedrooms honeymoon. Then I moved to the next scene.

5. *The appropriate transition*

When you choose a transition, think about what you want to achieve.

If your objective is only to move your characters from one time and place to another, if nothing of importance to your story has happened in between, use the transition that gets you smoothly from A to B with the fewest words: a double space, a chapter break, a word image, or a concept transition. If the reader needs an explanation, you can make the transition, then filter in details through character thoughts or dialogue in the next scene.

If you want the reader to arrive at the new scene with information about what happened in between, or if you want the reader to have a sense of passing time between scenes, use a narrative bridge.

No matter which transition method you use, always signal information about the new location in time, space, and character viewpoint as soon as you can after making the move.

20.

A strategy for revision

You want the first editor who reads your book to pick up the telephone and call you with an offer to buy. To help this dream come true, take the time now to examine every aspect of your novel, looking for ways to improve and polish.

a. Plot and sequence

Ask yourself whether the sequence of events makes sense. Does each step of your plot follow logically after the step before? Are your scenes in their natural order? Does it make sense for Mary to find out about Paul's ex-wife before they make love, or would it work better if she found out the morning after?

To check the sequence of events in your book:

(a) take a pile of flash cards;

(b) for each scene, write a few words on a flash card to identify that scene;

(c) sort the flash cards into order according to the sequence of events in your book; and

(d) read the cards, one after the other, asking yourself if the order of events is logical and natural.

If you're writing on computer, moving a scene is a simple matter of cutting the paragraphs from the original location, then pasting them to the new location. After moving text, be sure you reread both source and destination sections to catch inconsistencies created by the move.

b. Motivation

Readers will accept and sympathize with most character emotions and behaviors, *if* they have some understanding of why! It isn't always necessary to spell out the reason for each action, but your reader must believe there is a reason. To be fair to the reader, if you hint in chapter 3, for example, that Mary has a good reason for demanding Harry meet her at the drugstore instead of coming to her house, in chapter 4, 5, or 6, give the reader more details.

Review chapters 3 through 6 of this book, then ask yourself:

(a) What are your characters' goals for the time period of the novel?

(b) What are your characters' hang-ups and history?

(c) Knowing what you do about these people, does each character action and emotion make sense to you? Will it make sense to the reader?

If someone reads your story and comments, "I don't understand why the heroine did that," don't bother explaining. Go to your manuscript and make sure the motivation is clear. When your book is on the shelves, you won't have a chance to explain.

c. Setting

Reread chapter 7 of this book, then ask yourself:

(a) Does each scene give the reader a sense of place?

(b) Have you used action words in describing scenery (e.g., "The path meandered. The clouds threatened.")?

(c) Have you shown how your characters feel about their setting?

(d) If the setting is one that sharply affects the lives of your characters, have you shown the reader how much influence the setting has on characters, conflict, and story?

d. Character voice

Review chapter 14, then ask yourself:

(a) Does each of your characters speak in a unique way, consistent with background, gender, and self-concept?

(b) Does the reader always know who is speaking?

(c) Do your dialogue scenes include both speech and body language? Do your characters use meaningful body language? Check for characters who repeatedly shrug, grin, or nod.

(d) Does the reader learn at least one physical fact when first introduced to each character, to assist in forming a mental image of that character?

(e) What makes each character unique? What does each want? If two characters have similar goals, personalities, and voices, perhaps they perform the same function in your book. Consider removing one.

e. Suspense

Review chapter 16, then ask yourself:

(a) Do you create suspense by generating unanswered questions on the first page?

(b) Have you started your book at the beginning of the action, or before the beginning?

(c) Does your story open with the point-of-view character in a state of crisis or change? If not, could you start the story at chapter 2 and filter in necessary details from chapter 1? Could you start at chapter 3?

(d) Do you present new questions before you answer old ones for the reader? If not, rearrange events to create more suspense for your reader.

(e) Once the story question is answered, the reader has no motivation to keep reading. Do you withhold a complete answer to your story question until the end?

f. Pacing revisions

Review chapter 17, then examine your novel.

(a) Is each passage important to the novel? If not, it shouldn't be there. Search for, and eliminate, instances where you tell the reader something she already knows.

(b) Does each passage have emotional significance to the characters? If it's not important to the characters, it won't seem important to your reader.

(c) Does each passage contribute to the objective of the book by acting to make things either worse or better?

As you read your novel, ask yourself if any passage leaves you feeling confused or disoriented. You may need to take time to fill out your scenes to give the reader more of your characters' sensory information and insert brief sequels between scenes to allow the reader a bit of time to reflect on what went before.

g. *Point of view*

Review chapter 18, then ask yourself:

(a) In each passage, do you clearly signal viewpoint to the reader? If not, revise to sprinkle the passage lightly with thoughts, sights, sounds, scents, tastes, and touches experienced by your viewpoint character.

(b) Is every piece of information in the passage available to your viewpoint character? Eliminate any information that cannot be seen, heard, tasted, smelled, or felt by the viewpoint character. If you need the information, find another way to get it into the scene, for example, by using dialogue or a viewpoint shift. Take out negative viewpoint statements like: "Sam didn't see Jane take the twenty dollar bill from his wallet." If the viewpoint character didn't see it, don't tell the reader.

h. *Grammar and style*

If your grammar is rusty, you'll need to upgrade your skills. Most secretarial manuals include a clear description of basic grammar rules. Many community colleges have courses in business writing that provide an effective brush-up of grammar skills. One of the best grammar refreshers for writers is the Writer's Digest *Elements of Effective Writing* correspondence course. (See Appendix 3.)

Probably the best thing you can do to improve the effectiveness of your writing is to read and apply *The Elements of Style* by William Strunk, Jr., and E.B. White. This little book contains a wealth of concise guidelines for eliminating weak words and building solid sentence structure.

If you want to eliminate the drudgery of searching out these weak words, use a computer macro to highlight weak words. (See section **c.** in Appendix 3.) Whether you search your manuscript with pen and paper, or let your computer do the hard work, look for these things:

- **Shorter is better.** In general, if you can find a shorter way to say something without losing information, it will have more impact on the reader.

- **Think about pictures**. Your reader will be forming mental pictures based on the words you write. Try to make sure these pictures are vivid and clear.

- **Specific is better.** It's more powerful to say "It poured for 18 hours yesterday," than "It's been raining a lot lately." The reader forms a sharper mental image of "a dozen college students" than "a group of people"; a sharper image of "a Corvette" than "a car." Wherever you can, be specific.

- **"ing" verb forms describe unfinished actions.** "He fell" evokes a sharper picture than "he was falling." Use "ing" only when you wish to describe an uncompleted action or create a sense of timelessness.

- **Was, were, had, have.** Complex verb forms can often be shortened to simpler forms for more graphic reading. Substitute shorter forms (e.g., "gone" instead of "had gone") unless the change creates confusion.

- **That, that, and that**. Most of us use the word "that" more than necessary. Try searching for "that" on computer and removing it except where its absence causes confusion.

- **-ly.** Adverbs often weaken a sentence by distracting from the action verb. Where possible, use graphic verbs to eliminate the need for adverbs. "He went quickly to the store," is less graphic than "He hurried to the store," "He rushed to the store," or "He ran to the store." Use your computer to search for "ly."

- **Overused words.** Search for overused words such as "pretty," "nice," and "awful." By substituting more meaningful words, you'll give the reader a more graphic mental picture of what you're saying.

- **Qualifying words**. Eliminate qualifiers such as "almost," "very," and "quite." They dilute the reader's mental picture, and they usually aren't necessary. "He was quite tall" gives no more information than "He was tall." The second version leaves the reader with a sharper image.

- **Negatives.** Use your computer to search for "not" and "n't." Sentences containing negatives are often long and confusing. A negative describes something that isn't there, yet the reader can't visualize *nothing.* Change "He was not in favor of the new legislation" to "He disliked the new legislation."

i. A critic for your completed manuscript

When you've done everything you can to polish and prepare your manuscript for publication, you may feel you want someone else to evaluate it before you submit it to a publisher.

If you know a published writer who understands the romance genre, and whose work you respect, you might ask if that writer would be willing to read your first chapter. You can learn a lot from having one chapter evaluated, but be understanding if the author refuses. Evaluating even a chapter takes a significant amount of time.

If you join a chapter of the Romance Writers of America (RWA)(see Appendix 3), your chapter may have a critique clearing house or manuscript evaluation service. RWA and other writers groups have yearly contests for both published and unpublished writers. If you submit your manuscript to one of these, you may receive valuable feedback on your score sheets.

If you don't have access to either of these options, you can form a critique group with other developing writers to offer each other constructive criticism and support.

j. Finding a mentor

Many published writers in the romance field have mentored developing writers by giving workshops, offering advice, and reading and commenting on their manuscripts. The best way to find a mentor is probably to join a writers group where published writers form part of the membership. You'll meet many writers and have the opportunity to develop relationships with them.

If you're on the Internet, you can join any of several on-line writing workshops in which writers post their writing to the group for comment.

Don't share your work with anyone you don't feel comfortable with, and no matter how qualified your critic or mentor is, don't change your manuscript unless you yourself believe the change is right for your characters and your story. If you can't find a suitable mentor, or you feel uncomfortable about being mentored, carry on alone.

Don't change your manuscript unless you believe the change is right for your characters and story.

Part 5

Selling your romance novel

21.

Preparing for the marketplace

a. Publishers' guidelines

Most romance publishers have their own guidelines, referred to as publisher's guidelines, editorial guidelines, or tip sheets. To obtain a copy, look up the publisher's address on the copyright page of any book by that publisher or in a market guide (see Appendix 3 for a list of market guides). Then write the publisher, requesting publisher's guidelines for the lines you are interested in.

Whenever you send a submission to a publisher, enclose a self-addressed stamped envelope (SASE). If you submit material outside your own country, be sure to enclose international reply coupons (IRCs) sufficient to cover return postage, or buy stamps produced by the country you are sending to. Some writers groups provide a foreign stamp purchasing service for members.

If you're marketing a romance novel, I'd recommend you purchase the *Romance Writer's Pink Pages*. This romance market guide contains publishers' guidelines for dozens of romance lines, and it's updated yearly.

You'll have the best chance of selling your manuscript if you send it to the publisher whose guidelines most closely match your novel.

Check the word length in guidelines. If your novel is 65,000 words and you plan to submit it to Harlequin Presents which is asking for 55,000-word novels, don't do it! If you're determined your book is perfect for Harlequin Presents, go back and shorten it by 10,000 words

> **Whenever you communicate with a publisher, send a self-addressed stamped envelope for the reply.**

before you submit it. Otherwise, submit to a line with similar story requirements but a longer length requirement.

Your word processor probably has a function to count the words in your document. If not, you can get a word count by selecting three pages at random from the manuscript — not chapter beginning or ending pages. Count the number of words on all three pages, then divide the total by three. This is your average number of words per page. Multiply this by the number of pages in your manuscript. Because of chapter beginnings and endings, this will give you a word length that's a little high, but close enough to base manuscript submissions on.

b. Manuscript preparation

Your manuscript should be printed with a high-quality printer on white 8.5" by 11" bond paper (20 pound bond is standard). If the publisher's editorial guidelines include manuscript submission guidelines, follow them. If not, use the ones that follow:

(a) Do not right justify the print. Leave the right margin ragged, because right-justified print is harder to read and typeset.

(b) Font: choose a serif font such as Times Roman, rather than a sans serif such as Helvetica or Arial. Serif fonts are easier to read.

(c) Margins: leave at least one-inch margins all around the page.

(d) Your manuscript should have a cover page, similar to that shown in Sample #5.

(e) Header: On every page beginning with page 2, include a page header with the title and page number. You may also include your name in brackets if you wish. Don't use any other header or footer.

(f) Chapters: At the beginning of every chapter, center the chapter title one third of the way down the page. After the chapter title, double space before the first paragraph.

(g) Text: Each paragraph should begin with a half-inch indent. Text should be double spaced, with no additional space between paragraphs, except at breaks.

(h) Breaks: Indicate a significant break within a chapter for a point-of-view shift or a shift in time or setting by one of the following methods:

(i) Leave an additional blank line between paragraphs, then begin the new section with no indent on the first paragraph.

(ii) At the end of the paragraph before the break, make a carriage return. Then type between one and three asterisks on the next line. Center the line of asterisks. Type another carriage return and begin the next paragraph with normal indent.

c. The marketplace

The process of revising your manuscript should bring it as close to perfection as you can achieve. Now you're ready to send your manuscript to a publisher or literary agent.

Sample #5
Manuscript Format

The Moon Lady's Lover

by

Vanessa Grant

Vanessa Grant
Box 1234
Anywhere, BC V0T 1Z0
CANADA
Phone (250) 555-1214

CHAPTER ONE

When the jet landed in Vancouver, Cynthia Dyson-Paige was still rehearsing what she would say to Jonathan Halley. She'd been practicing the words all through the four hour flight from Toronto.

She rented a car at the airport, wincing as her credit card went through the imprinting machine. Then she crawled into Vancouver with the morning rush hour traffic, still rehearsing the encounter to come.

I thought you'd want to help Allan. He needs help...

She tried to hear Jonathan's response in her mind but that part of the conversation was a blank. She knew it was outrageous that she should come to him like this, ridiculous to think she could ask him for help when they hadn't spoken a civil word in the fourteen years since she was sixteen.

There were no other options.

I came to ask you for money...

Since yesterday she'd spent hours fantasizing how it would be. He wouldn't smile when he saw her. She hadn't called to say she was coming, so he wouldn't be expecting her. He'd look up from his desk in that high rise building in Vancouver's financial district and both his mouth and his eyes would frown.

Three months ago she'd seen pictures in a magazine article and she knew the decor of his office, even the scope of the ocean view out the window. So when she said silently, Jonathan, I need help, her mind instantly provided the surroundings from the magazine pictures.

It hadn't occurred to her that he wouldn't be there, but at nine-thirty she was thirteen stories above the ground listening to a well groomed female dragon tell her that Mr. Halley was out of town.

"Where is he?" If he was in Toronto it would be ironic because she'd just flown across the continent searching for him. But better Toronto than Europe because she might not be able to get an immediate overseas flight.

She couldn't afford to waste a day.

The dragon frowned under iron-tidy hair but it seemed Jonathan's movements weren't secret because she said, "On Vancouver Island. A little village called Parkland."

Oh, God ...

When her father's estate was wound up Cynthia had seen Jonathan's name on the Agreement for Sale for the Parkland estate. She

22.

Going to market

Your romance novel is polished and printed in clear type on good bond paper. Should you send it to your favorite romance publisher? Should you use a literary agent? Is there a secret to selling a romance, or is it enough to have a good book?

a. Do you need a literary agent?

A literary agent represents an author's work, presenting it to possible publishers on the author's behalf. If the publisher is interested in purchasing the novel, the agent consults with the author, then negotiates a contract for the sale on the author's behalf. In return for these services, the agent takes a percentage of the writer's royalties — usually 15% for domestic sales, and a higher percentage for foreign sales. Many agents also charge for disbursements such as photocopying and long distance telephone calls.

A good agent can be invaluable. He or she will know the literary market well and be on speaking terms with several possible editors for your novel. When the publisher offers a contract, a good agent will be in a position to judge how the contract compares to those offered other authors.

Through the course of your career, you may deal with many editors. If you establish a mutually beneficial relationship with an agent, you'll have someone to give you advice, support, and help in working toward your long-term writing goals.

Many writers compare the relationship between an author and a literary agent to a marriage. When it works well, you and your agent

Carolyn Swayze on...An Agent's Ideal Writer

The agent tingled with expectancy. The purposive and confident stride of the darkly handsome man approaching her suggested that he intended to give her total satisfaction. "Are you the literary agent?" he whispered intimately. Breathless with anticipation, she could only nod in acquiescence. "I hear you've been longing for something special," the postal worker murmured, swinging his muscular arm from behind his broad back to triumphantly display a plain brown envelope.

Tremulously, scarcely daring to believe that it had come at last, she reached for it. Too needy to hide her deep throbbing desire, she tore open the slim packet. Yes! It was all there: a one-page letter introducing the author, a brief synopsis and the first few (double-spaced) chapters of a thrilling romance novel, *Be Still My Beating Heart*, and — oh, joy — a self-addressed stamped envelope. She twirled away on dancing feet, eager to read and savor this treat.

"Hey," the forgotten man called out. "What about me? I've been writing a novel, too. It's about this guy who..."

"Sorry," she dismissed him disdainfully, "I don't take verbal inquiries."

...

With a little luck, this agent would read a strongly written, letter-perfect manuscript which she would be proud to represent, while honestly assuring the author that she has knowledge, expertise, interest, and connections in romance novel publishing. Once an agency agreement has been made, and when both agent and author are satisfied that the manuscript is as good as it can possibly be, they will collaborate on initial submissions.

At that point, the perfect client will start working on the next book. The dutiful agent will apprise the author of submissions and responses. The ideal author will trust that her agent is advancing her work at every opportunity. She will accept that if an agent is always in the office answering her phone calls and letters and providing editorial input, she cannot be actively marketing her work or the work of others.

They will appreciate one another and celebrate their successes.

They will live happily ever after.

are partners working for your mutual benefit. Because you are confident your agent is doing the best for you, you can leave your book in your agent's hands and get on with writing your next novel, knowing the agent is promoting your work effectively at every opportunity. However, when the relationship between author and agent breaks down, it may feel like a disastrous marriage filled with resentment and distrust.

When the writer-agent relationship fails, often it's because writer and agent have different ideas about each other's duties. Most literary agents represent a number of writers and must balance the needs of each writer against the time available. An agent's duties include networking with publishers, keeping up with current trends in fiction, constantly researching the market, promoting authors to publishers, evaluating and negotiating contracts, reading and evaluating author's manuscripts, and advising authors.

Before you make an agreement with an agent, be sure you and the agent have the same ideas about the amount of contact that will take place between you, and about both author's and agent's duties in the relationship. Ask the agent for references, and do check them.

If you're searching for a literary agent, read the current edition of the Writer's Digest Books *Guide to Literary Agents*. In addition to providing names, addresses, and areas of interest for hundreds of literary agents, the *Guide* includes articles by writers and agents about what to expect from the writer-agent relationship and a wealth of information on how to go about finding an agent and what to expect when you get one.

b. Selling your novel directly to a publisher

Most publishers of category romance accept manuscripts from writers without an agent, and many writers have sold novels without an agent. If your manuscript is a single-title romance, it's more difficult. Some single-title editors will not read unagented submissions unless they've been invited. (For details on category and single-title publishers that accept direct submissions, read the *Romance Writer's Pink Pages* and the Romance Writers of America market updates, published in the RWA members' magazine.)

1. Invitation to submit
If you believe your manuscript is suitable for a certain publisher, try to obtain an invitation to submit it to that publisher. If you attend a

> Be sure you and your prospective literary agent have the same idea about the amount of contact that will take place between you.

> Most category romance publishers accept manuscripts from writers without an agent.

writer's conference where you have the opportunity to tell a suitable editor you've written a novel you believe she'd like, you may be invited to submit your manuscript. If you attend a workshop given by an editor, you can write to her saying you attended her workshop and you believe your novel is exactly what she is looking for. Use the query letter format shown in Sample #6. Such a letter will sometimes result in an invitation to submit.

Otherwise, the best way to get an invitation to submit is to write a great query letter.

2. Query letters

When you've completed the first draft of your novel, write a query letter to several publishers you think your manuscript could be suitable for. Your query should be no more than one page long. In the first paragraph, describe the concept of your book, focusing on the conflict issue between your characters. In the second paragraph, describe your qualifications to write about the subject matter, and any writing credits you may have. Then ask if the editor would like to see your novel. Be sure to include a SASE with your query letter.

3. The book synopsis

> A synopsis should always be written in the present tense.

Some publishers' editorial guidelines request writers to send a synopsis or outline of their novel with the query letter or with the manuscript. Others ask for a proposal consisting of a synopsis and a specified number of sample chapters.

A synopsis or outline of your book should describe the general events of the book in narrative form. A synopsis should always be written in the present tense. Publishers' guidelines sometimes specify the length a synopsis should be. Some editors want to see a brief 2-page summary of the novel, while others want a detailed 20-page summary. If length isn't specified, try to keep yours to no more than 10 or 12 double-spaced pages. When writing your synopsis, focus on the conflict between the characters, and the development of their romantic relationship.

Sample #7 displays a synopsis by Judy Griffith Gill.

Sample #6
Query Letter

Jane Writer
123 Any Street
Anywhere, AA 19876
Phone: (604) 555-1234
Fax: (604) 555-5432

Harold Sawerson, Senior Editor
Romance Books
678 5th Avenue
New York, New York
18977 USA

July 1, 199-

Dear Mr. Sawerson:

Marnie Jones is a passionate artist who needs an isolated, natural environment for her painting. After a disastrous two years in the city, she's now moved to a West Coast lighthouse where she's fulfilled as an artist, and she vows never to leave. But Marnie's life is thrown into chaos when she falls in love with New York stockbroker Scott Trainer. She must choose between her lifetime passion for her art and the man she loves.

I've just described the central conflict of my romance novel, *Island Affair*, set on a west coast Canadian lighthouse. Like the heroine, I'm a painter who works in oils. I'm familiar with lighthouse settings, as I lived on a British Columbia lighthouse station for six years.

I'm excited about *Island Affair* and I believe it's perfect for your The Ultimate Romance line. May I submit a copy of the manuscript to you?

Yours sincerely,

Jane Writer

Jane Writer

Sample #7
A Synopsis by Judy Griffith Gill

There's Something About the Nanny

by

Judy Griffith Gill

Synopsis

Alan Magnus needs a nanny for his motherless four-year-old, Deanna. Deanna, for her part, would rather have a fairy. When Alan looks out into his backyard and sees a strange woman with Deanna, he immediately jumps to conclusions — the main one being that his daughter's maternal grandparents have sent her to snatch the little girl, as they have threatened to do. He confronts the woman, and tells her to leave. Deanna, who has clearly accepted the stranger already as her new nanny, wants the woman to stay.

While Alan has wanted an older, grandmotherly nanny, and finds himself much too attracted to this woman with the purple eyes, she's the only nanny candidate to whom Deanna has taken. Since he has a looming deadline on his book revisions, he hires her despite his misgivings. He's confident the employment agency wouldn't have sent someone who hadn't been thoroughly vetted. He's delighted to have someone — anyone — to entertain his daughter. He'll never be far from them, so he can make certain this Misty Fawkes is what she says she is — or preferably, not what she says she is.

She says she's an elf.

Misty — Elf of the Morning Mist — is unable to lie. If she's asked a direct question, she must answer truthfully, so when Alan Magnus asks her, she is obliged to tell him her name. She knows he doesn't believe her, but there is nothing she can do about that. She has an assignment — fixing up Alan and Deanna's lives. Deanna called for a fairy, but the Mother of All had none available, and sent Misty. Once an elf has accepted such a mission, she cannot leave it unless the person who invoked her releases her, and she doesn't think Deanna is about to do that. She knows she doesn't have to fulfill her duties in the form of a nanny, but it seems the most logical thing to do, since a nanny is needed on the scene.

She intends to make this a quick, in-and-out job; find a mother-replacement for Deanna, a wife for Alan. Once that's completed, she can return to the Upper World with a success story behind her. Her last mission was a failure, and she has something to prove — mostly to herself. When she finds herself attracted to Alan, she suspects the Mother of All of interfering with her life. The Mother likes her creatures to do terms as mortals once in a while to keep them balanced and make them more compassionate. Misty has utterly no intention of complying.

The Mother can't force her to do it; she can advise, and all too often does, but elves enjoy an autonomy the Mother can't quite accept. She tries to circumvent that by trickery.

Misty is determined to elude any kind of web the Mother might cast around her because if an elf falls in love with a mortal man who doesn't believe in elves and fairies, she loses her powers. This is not an easy thought for Misty to contemplate. She likes being an elf. Likes being free to come and go anywhere and anywhen. But she also likes Deanna. And Alan. She likes Alan far too much, and knows he's beginning to feel the same toward her. The man, whether he's willing it admit it or not, can see visions, and Misty's over-active imagination creates too many of them that she and Alan share. He pretends to ignore them, but she knows he's seen the one of two bodies lying warm and tangled on a mussed bed, the one of a breakfast table set for two, and other erotic fantasies that arise from her mind. She isn't sure if this is a result of the Mother's interference or her own slipping faculties, but she does know she's in grave danger and has to hurry, to get out before she's all caught up in an impossible situation.

Though Alan does, as a result of Misty's insistence as well as his desire to get away from her before she drives him to distraction, date women, he finds them not to his liking. He's never been much of a socializer anyway; his relationship with Deanna's mother being the only one of any significance. It was short, physical, and intense, and she left him without a hint of her pregnancy. Indeed, Alan has only in recent months learned of his fatherhood, following the death of Deanna's mother. He thinks he's forgotten how to be a good date, a good companion to a woman — except with Misty. They get along all too well, try as they both do to curtail their attraction to each other. It gets worse when he takes it upon himself to teach her to drive.

His kisses are far more magical than they should be, considering he is a mortal man and Misty soon knows she's in very serious trouble. She is falling in love with a man who doesn't believe. She could leave, she knows. There is still time. Just barely, but time. All she needs to do is ask Deanna to release her from her bond. She could tell Deanna that her time on Earth is done, that she has been called home. She could explain it in such a way that the child would understand, and willingly say the magic words required to free Misty.

But…her time on Earth is not done. She has not completed her task, and the Mother has not called her back. Elves do not lie, and neither do they renege. Misty can't bear the thought of returning to the Upper World to report another failure to the Mother of All. She must stay and see this through, one way or another, to its end.

When Alan realizes he's a gone goose over a woman who not only pretends to be an elf, but whom he suspects seriously believes it, he's appalled. He's always prided himself on being a pragmatic realist, although he makes his living writing fiction. How can he love a woman who is clearly a nut-case? But he does. More and more each day. He wants her in his life forever. He needs her. Deanna needs her. And, he believes, she needs them to keep her at least partially rooted in reality.

The first time Misty invites him into her rooms and he sees the changes she has wrought, he begins to doubt his own sanity, too. He sees, or thinks he sees, a brook emerging from a small stand of trees in one corner, spilling into a silver pool with bright green and gold fish, then seeming to disappear into the fabric of the carpet. Birds flit and twitter, and butterflies dance over bright blossoms. And that's just in her sitting room.

Her bedroom is something else again, and by the time morning comes, he is so close to believing in magic that it scares him. His resolve stiffens. He must make Misty see the truth of the matter, must make her admit it to him as well as to herself. She might be a master of sleight of hand, perhaps she's even an incredibly talented hypnotist, but she is not an elf. She cannot be. Elves do not exist. Even her forest glade and trickling brook, her birds and butterflies have not lasted the night. They had been a figment of her imagination — and to his shame, his. But she exists, and he loves her. He can't let her go. He won't.

After her first night with Alan, Misty knows she is lost. She has done the unthinkable. She has traded her magic for the love of a disbelieving man. She doesn't think she can live this way. Their first breakfast together, when she tries to replicate a vision her mind had once conjured up, and that she knows Alan shared, proves it.

She doesn't know how to cook. When the time comes to get changed from Alan's shirt and dress into her own clothes, she has none —and can conjure up none.

Alan can't understand Misty's sudden inability to do any of the things at which she's been so competent for the past month or so. Nor can he understand why she can't find any of her clothes. He's sure, when he checks her closet for himself, that they've suffered a break-in and is all for calling the law. Misty is clearly against that, so he takes her shopping. That, too, is more fun than he could have dreamed, and he falls even more deeply in love.

Misty, to her surprise, enjoys the shopping trip. She resolves to make the best of things. She may not have magic at her fingertips, but she has Alan and Deanna in her life. Yet in the back of her mind lies the memory of the way it used to be, the way she had thought it would always be. If only Alan could believe, then she could have it all.

When Deanna runs out onto the road and Misty can't save her by magical means, she does the only thing possible, saves her by human means, and Deanna is still hurt, though not badly. Sick with grief over her incompetence as a human, Misty does the only thing she can do — she asks Deanna to let her go. Deanna, not fully understanding, does so.

She returns to the Upper World to watch over Deanna and Alan from there. Yet, watching them, seeing their sadness at her departure, feeling the lack of joy with which she performs her tasks, she wonders if she has made the right decision. Is it worth being an elf, and residing in the Upper World, with all its delights, if she has to give up the family she loves? The answer is no. She must go back. She can and will learn to live without her magical powers, because there is greater power and magic in love.

Alan can't believe Misty has left them so unceremoniously. He maintains a deep belief that there is one true mate for each person, and that in Misty he had found his. How could she leave him? He knows she loved him, knows she loved Deanna. Deanna has the answer, but he doesn't want to hear it, doesn't want to know that his failure to believe in Misty cost her her powers. Yet, as the days and nights pass, he realizes he can't go on without her.

Looking up at the night sky, he says the magic words Deanna has told him he must in order to get Misty back. To his shock and joy, Misty appears before him. This time, he is the one who has invoked her magic. This time, it is he to whom she must belong — until he agrees to release her. Which, he tells her, he will never do.

Back on Earth, in the arms of a man who now believes, Misty's magic returns to her. She discovers that a term as a mortal (although one with extraordinary powers) is exactly what she wants.

c. Submission and response

By the time you've completed your revisions, you may have an invitation in response to one of your query letters. Print your manuscript with a good printer, put a suitable elastic around it, and place it carefully into a tough, padded envelope or a box. If the editor asks you to send an outline of your book in addition to the manuscript, include the outline with the manuscript. Write a cover letter for the manuscript, addressed to the editor who requested it. This letter should be very short, referring to the editor's invitation letter and mentioning what you've enclosed (your manuscript, or manuscript and outline). Be sure to enclose a SASE and mark the envelope "Requested material."

The publisher's tip sheets may have given an estimate of the length of time you can expect to wait for a reply. Many publishers take several months to reply to a manuscript submission. If the expected time has elapsed and you haven't heard, write a short query letter asking about the status of your book.

If the publisher returns your manuscript with a rejection letter, read it carefully. If you received a form letter as a rejection, don't be discouraged. Another editor may think it's perfect for his or her line. If an editor comments on problems in your book, consider whether you agree with the criticism. If you do agree and you're willing to revise your novel, write the editor expressing thanks for the useful constructive criticism and ask if the editor would like to see the manuscript again if you revise it to deal with these problems. Many writers have used this proactive technique to turn a rejection into an invitation to resubmit.

Receiving a rejection of your novel can be a shattering experience. It's important to realize that a rejection does not necessarily mean your book isn't good, only that it isn't the story this editor is looking for.

If you know other supportive writers, share your disappointment with them. Talk to friends, lovers, anyone who will affirm that you are a good person and a good writer. Rant and rave a little, shed a few tears, then get your manuscript off to another publisher and carry on writing the next one.

It may take longer than you expected to get published, but remember this: the writers who get published are the ones who keep writing, submitting, and working to make their writing better.

Appendix 1
Yesterday's Vows —
book notes

The pages that follow contain the book notes I developed for *Yesterday's Vows*. The document template that I use is available in Microsoft Word for Windows, Amipro, and Corel WordPerfect format from Dogwood Technical Services Inc. (See section **c.** in Appendix 3.)

Experiment with your own notes format, changing it to find what works best for you.

Manuscript Data Sheet

TITLE: Yesterday's Vows   **BY:** Vanessa Grant

Setting: San Diego/Ensenada area and Thetis Island (B.C., Canada)

Duration: 3 weeks, May

Main Conflict: If Connar Stanfield ever finds his runaway wife, he wants two things from her — an explanation and a divorce. He married Dixie partly to satisfy a promise to her father and partly because she'd grown into a very desirable woman. But Dixie fled within a day of the wedding ceremony and Connar has spent seven years worrying because he doesn't believe she's a girl who can fend for herself. But the woman Connar finally finds is anything but helpless and it doesn't take him long to realize that letting her go again is the last thing he wants. The trouble is, Dixie Bradshaw believes that marrying Connar was the most foolish thing she's ever done. Once she loved him desperately...but never again! Yet how can she deny him the right to know his own child?

HEROINE: Dixie Bradshaw

Age: 27, looks younger

Occupation: artist

Character: Artistic and impulsive woman with a very strong will beneath a fragile appearance. She's determined to control her own life and not let anyone hurt her again.

Ht/Body Type: 5 ft, 6 in; slender flowing curves; seems insubstantial; fine bone structure

Hair: Dark brown, glints red in the sun, cut in a pixie cut. Hair was long and wavy 7 years ago, so much hair that she seemed even more insubstantial.

Eye Color: chocolate brown

HERO: Connar Stanford

Age: 34

Occupation: television broadcaster, writer

Character: strong-willed, ambitious, hot temper firmly leashed, fights for what he believes in, impulsive

Ht/Body Type: 6 ft, lean, muscular

Hair: unruly, sandy blonde

Eye Color: blue

TIME LINE

Year	Age of Heroine	Age of Hero	Event
1993, May 8	27	34	Chapter 1, Connar arrives at Dixie's exhibit
1993, May 1	27	34	Connar sees a picture of Dixie on back of her print in his network chief's office
1991	25	32	Connar disappears in Central America, reappears a week later with footage that breaks open a large drug smuggling ring
1989	23	30	Connar disappears in South Africa, reappears 2 weeks later with more incredible footage
1988	22	29	Connar disappears in Lebanon, reappears 3 months later with incredible footage of terrorists
1987, June 30	21	28	Dixie's baby, Jess Bradshaw, born in Ensenada, Dixie would have graduated from art school if she'd not run from Connar
1986, Oct 8	20	27	Dixie runs away from Connar
1986, Oct 7	20	27	Dixie and Connar married by Vancouver marriage commissioner
1986, Sept 30	20	27	Devlin died from stray bullet covering a terrorist kidnapping in Paris. Connar was working with him. Dev's last wish was for Connar to look after Dixie. "I never looked after her the way I should have. Always wished I'd been a better father..."
1986, April	20	27	Foster mother Jessie Stanford died. Dixie spent that summer working at a gallery in Vancouver
1983	17	24	Dixie's father was in Paris. Dixie entered art school near her grandfather's
1981, May	15	22	Connar graduated and went to work for Continental News
1980, Dec 7	15	21	Dixie ran away when her father called on her birthday canceling her trip to see him in Paris, Conn found her and talked her back
1977, summer	11	18	Conn home from college, finds Dixie's hiding place in the old cabin by beach
1973	6	13	Dixie's mother dies, Dixie goes to live with Connar and his mother — calls her Aunt Jessie
1965, Dec 7	0	7	Dixie born
1958, Dec 25		0	Connar born, son of Jessie Stanford

CHAPTERS

Chap	Words	Date/Day	Event
1	5037	May 8, 1993	Conn arrives at Dixie's display in San Diego. Conn's POV, flash to he sees Dixie's picture in network chief's office
2	4269	May 8, 1993	Dixie meets Connar at Shelter Island
3	4951	1973–86	Flashback, from Dixie's coming to Aunt Jessie's, to Devlin's death
4	4542	1986	Flashback, from funeral and marriage, to the edge of making love on wedding night
5	5324	May 10, 1993	Dixie remembers wedding night on way to the mall, then encounters Connar; Mexican stand-off with Wolf growling at Conn
6	6266	May 10, Mon	Dixie, Conn, and Wolf to hamburger stand, Dixie tells Conn about their child Jess
7	6516	May 10, Mon	Connar meets Jess and tells Dixie they're coming home with him
8	5283	May 16–17	On Thetis Island
9	4749	May 17–21	Lazy days, countdown to black moment. Conn makes love to Dixie
10	6836	May 21	Black moment and resolution
Total	53773		

HEROINE: *Dixie Bradshaw*

Born December 7, 1965

History, prime motivating force, prime motivating event

Daughter of Devlin Bradshaw and Sally Bradshaw. Sally died when Dixie was 6. Devlin was a television news correspondent. Sally and daughter traveled everywhere with him. When Sally died Devlin came home and, neither he nor Sally having close family, left Dixie with Jessie Stanford and her young son Connar on Thetis Island.

She's always been gullible. Believed her father when he said he'd be back for Christmas. When Connar said they should get married, she believed he loved her. Believed she'd get to go with him, not be left behind.

Dixie's prime motivating force — "I'm never going to be any-body's cast off again. Nobody will have the power to leave me behind." Control and independence.

History with Connar

Dixie worshipped Connar from the moment she came to live with Jessie. She married him, threw herself at him and then learned he planned to leave her behind. When she demands to know why he married her, she discovers he promised her father he'd look after her. It's the ultimate betrayal. Her father was never her father and Connar will never be her husband. She has a deep anger against her father. As for Connar, she sees her future as his wife, watching on the news while he dies too, knowing he doesn't love her. She runs from the marriage.

For years she imagined he would come to find her. He'd always been the responsible one. The one who was there when everyone else faded away. In the first year after she ran, she thought about him all the time, knowing he'd be determined to look after her, to find her. But the year passed and she got things in perspective. She didn't plan to stay in Mexico. That just happened.

Until she left Connar, she was always dependent on other people for love and home and security. She was always gullible enough to believe they would give her what she needed. But she always got left behind. By her father. By Connar who said "marry me" but didn't mean what marriage was supposed to mean.

Now she's her own person with her own life and although she runs when Connar comes, she quickly decides she must go back and talk to him. But what about Jessie? And what about the fact that although Connar tells her he wants freedom from the marriage, and she offers him exactly that, he doesn't seem to want to let her go.

Work and ambitions

Dixie went to art college three years. She wanted to return to Thetis Island to be an artist there, never expected her foster mother Jessie to die. When Jessie died the summer Dixie was 20, she felt her roots had been torn away. Her father contacted her, obviously confused about what to do with her. She told him she was fine, she had a summer job in a Vancouver gallery. Then her father died in September. She was still in art college, had enough money to finish from his insurance but not much left over. Then Connar swept down and took over her life, married her and prepared to abandon her. He must have assumed she'd need someone to support her.

Worked as a waitress in San Diego after she left Connar, afraid to work in a gallery because Conn would look in galleries. Then she realized she was pregnant and was paranoid Conn would find her through the birth records. Met Sue who came in every morning for breakfast, grieving for husband and uneasy about living alone in Mexico. When Dixie confided her problem, she and Sue joined forces. Sue hired her as a maid — room and board and a few dollars. Sue really wanted someone to live with her, to enable her to feel comfortable staying in Mexico after her husband's death. Dixie had her daughter Jess there, in the guest house near the water that was her quarters. She walked the beach and started doing portraits of people on the beach.

Then bit by bit she built up a name for herself. Stopped being a maid and rented the guest house from Sue. She lives in Mexico, sells art in Ensenada and the States. She paints all winter and takes her stuff up to the States in May. She's made a deal with Ernie who sells artisans' work in the malls.

Dixie's home

She lives in Sue's cottage, pays rent. The cottage is on a cliff overlooking the sea, behind the house. Dixie knows decision time is coming for her, because Jessie should go to school this September. Where?

HERO: Connar Stanfield

Born December 25, 1958

History, prime motivating force, prime motivating event

Prime motivating event is lack of a father, and not knowing who his father is. Dixie's father became his hero. He wanted to be a correspondent like Devlin. He dreamed of it and when he went to university he planned to go on to broadcasting school. Connar felt closed in on the island, dreamed of being in the news, making the news. Getting away was his first priority. He was with Devlin when he died and he promised Dev he'd look after Dixie. He failed to keep that promise and it bothers him. He sees Dev more realistically now, but still feels guilt about failing to keep his promise.

Prime motivating force: the need to know the truth.

History with Dixie

He married Dixie partly to look after her but mostly because he didn't have time to work out her future before heading back to Europe. He had promised Dev. He decided to marry her, put her in the cottage. She could paint and live on money he sent. He thought he could marry her and give her a home, then they'd develop a relationship later. If it didn't work out they could get a divorce. He realizes now that the marriage was one of his more stupid ideas, and wonders what his motives really were. He never divorced her, although he did go out with a woman for a year and broke off with her because he couldn't take the step of terminating his marriage without first finding Dixie.

He wonders if she's alive and he wants to feel OK about her, but he worries. He's hired a private detective and gotten nowhere. His search efforts have slowed over the years and mainly he feels guilt over her. He wishes he'd done things differently in his relationship with Dixie.

Work and ambitions

Connar was the golden boy of the media. Hard hitting and courageous, he disappeared more than once while he was reporting in a war zone. He always turned up again and when he did he had the scoop. But his god was truth and too often he saw truth distorted by the media. He was promoted to a New York studio job, but soon quit because his hands were tied by union job descriptions. Reading other people's news to management criteria wasn't his bag. He signed a contract for a book blasting the media. To write it, he returned to live to the island where he grew up.

Connar's home

His great-grandfather homesteaded the farm on Thetis Island. When his grandpa died of a heart attack, his mother Jessie hired a neighbor to help work the farm, but she stayed on in the farmhouse overlooking the water. After Jessie's death Conn leased the farm out. He had a cottage built on the property for himself but seldom went there because of the memories. It's the home of his heart though, and last year he went there to work on the book. He'd like a home, roots, but Dixie is the nagging loose end in his past.

Characters, other — non point of view

Ernie (Ernest Carter)

Operates Embarcadero Artisans, a traveling gallery selling the works of various artists in Southern California. He's Dixie's agent. He's 40, short and bulky, looks like an artist himself, rough spoken but capable of charming anyone he cares to. A good friend but Dixie hasn't told him the truth about her. Unruly hair, faraway look in eyes, heavy brows.

Wolf (dog)

Five-year-old mongrel that looks like an arctic wolf. Dixie adopted him in Mexico when he was a puppy and she's trained him to a fine obedience. He's fiercely protective. He sleeps by Jess's bed and growls at men who get too close to either Dixie or Jess. Dixie doesn't feed him junk food because she promised him a decent diet.

Jessie Stanford (Connar's mother)

Jessie was 35 at the time Dixie came to live with her, never married after having Connar. Lived with her father, Conn's grandfather. When he died Jessie hired a neighbor to work the farm and lived in the house with Connar. She died the same year Devlin did, in the spring, without ever having told Conn a word about his father. She left Connar the farm.

Jess Bradshaw

Born June 30, 1987. She'll be six soon. Dixie's coloring and Connar's eyes, hair cut in short cap. She's eloquent, vocal, and not shy. Bilingual in Spanish and English.

Yvonne and Wayne Stannish

They've leased the farm for last few years. Have two seven-year-old grandchildren: twins Gary and Wendy. Twins have a playhouse up the hill from Connar's waterfront home, near old farmhouse Stannishes live in.

Tom Gaylie

Connar's New York network chief, spends lunch at nearby art gallery, ulcers, and high blood pressure, graying hair, deep lines of strain. Makes secretaries and reporters tremble.

Sue

Dixie's landlady, early thirties, fiery red long hair, manicured fingers, limp and must use a cane, from accident six-and-a-half years ago that killed husband Brett. They bought cliff-hanging house south of Mexican border together in early days of marriage, talked about retiring there one day. Sue met Dixie after Brett's death and made a deal with Dixie to come work for her as helper and use guest cottage. After Jess was born, Dixie stayed, rented cottage from Sue once she could afford to from sales of her art. Sue is like a big sister to her, aunt to Jess.

Jason Ellers

Law student who looked like Connar, Dixie tried to fall in love with him and was briefly engaged to him in her third year art school

Evan Collinson (wife Masie)

Conn hired him to look after farm after his mother's death.

Threads —
conflicts running through the story

Initial conflict

Connar wants to resolve the loose end of his marriage to Dixie. He needs to know what happened to her. He wants to resolve his sense of failure in his promise to Devlin. Marriage didn't matter to him when he married Dixie, that was supposed to be for her, or for Devlin. Now it matters. He wants to feel free to find a wife, to have children. He's been wandering for years and he's tired. He wants to put down roots but his past is a tangle.

Dixie is afraid of facing Connar, afraid she'll find she still loves him, afraid of being weak in the face of his strength, knows he'll want to do "the right thing" and have Jess as his daughter. She's built her own life on her own terms, but sometimes she aches for Connar, still hurts from his failure to love her.

Developing conflict

Dixie sees Connar as the man he was, refuses to see the changes in him. As she resolves to be free of him, he develops the need to have her back. His masculine pride is pricked by her ability to resist him when he comes on to her. He's seeing her as a new person, a strong and passionate but basically loving person, the woman of his dreams. When he discovers she's had his child, he vows no child of his will grow up without a father. He wants to legitimize the marriage, but Dixie's afraid to be caught again, to become his leftover, left behind when he goes out to live. She fears loving him and seeing his death on television as she did her father's. Conn, meanwhile, realizes Dixie is everything he's ever dreamed of in a lover, a partner.

MAY 1993

SUNDAY	MONDAY	TUESDAY	WEDNESDAY	THURSDAY	FRIDAY	SATURDAY
						1 *Ch.1 Connor sees Dixie's painting in his boss's office*
2	**3**	**4**	**5**	**6**	**7**	**8** *Ch.1 C at D's exhibit in San Diego. Ch. 2 D meets C*
9 *Mother's Day*	**10** *Ch. 5 to 7 Back to mall, with C picnic. C meets Jess.*	**11** *Ch. 5 to 7 C to D's*	**12**	**13**	**14**	**15**
16 *Ch. 8 Fly to Vancouver, to Thetis Island*	**17** *Thetis Island*	**18** *Ch. 9 Sketch C*	**19** *Ch. 9 Swimming*	**20** *Ch.9 Can I read your book?*	**21** *Ch. 9 2 days left, walk, make love*	**22** *Ch. 10 Black moment*
23	**24**	**25**	**26**	**27**	**28**	**29**
30	**31**					

Appendix 2
The category romance market

a. Categories of romances

Here is a description of the major divisions within the category romance market. For information on specific publishers, read the market information section of the Romance Writers of America's bimonthly magazine or consult a romance market guide such as the *Romance Writer's Pink Pages*.

Watch booksellers' offerings for signs of new categories and categories that aren't described here (e.g., fantasy and science fiction romance, paranormal romance, and ethnic romance). New categories are constantly emerging. Some become established and endure, while others are published for a few months and cease to exist.

Each of the divisions below also occurs in single-title romances.

1. Traditional romance

This category is the closest to the stereotypical Harlequin Romance of decades ago. The hero and heroine should be believable modern people with conventional values, who develop a conventional relationship. This category has the most rules. No sex outside marriage, and no graphic sex in the book. The action and conflict center closely around hero and heroine. The point of view is primarily the heroine's. (Silhouette Romance, Harlequin Romance, Harlequin Mills & Boon, Avalon Books)

2. Contemporary

Contemporary romance novels feature modern women with modern outlooks. Contemporary category romance publishers are the most likely to be interested in a book dealing with controversial issues or the paranormal.

Heroines in contemporary romances are independent women with a strong sense of who they are. The heroes may be old-fashioned or modern, but if they try to dominate the heroines they won't have an easy time of it. Many contemporary romances focus on the conflict between strong-willed men and independent women.

The short contemporary romance focuses primarily on hero and heroine. (Harlequin Presents, Harlequin Mills & Boon, Harlequin Temptation, Silhouette Desire, Bantam Loveswept)

The long contemporary romance may have well-developed subplots involving other characters. (Harlequin Superromance, Silhouette Special Edition, Silhouette Intimate Moments)

In contemporary romances, the hero and heroine usually consummate their sexual relationship in the book. Love scenes should be romantic rather than graphic. Some contemporary lines focus strongly on the physical desire between hero and heroine, and consummation of the relationship is expected in these novels. (Harlequin Temptation, Silhouette Desire)

3. Time travel, fantasy, and futuristic

These books blend romance with fantasy or science fiction. Many publishers have included them in their contemporary lines. Sensuality levels in these novels tends to be similar to contemporary romances. (Leisure Books, Harlequin Temptation, Harlequin Superromance)

4. Intrigue

In these books the heroine is enmeshed in a mystery while falling in love. The pace should be fast, with an atmosphere of suspense and danger. The balance between mystery and romance is hard to pull off, but when well done, this balance of intrigue and romance makes a great read. Intrigue publishers are always looking for new writers. (Harlequin Intrigue, some Silhouette Intimate Moments)

5. Historical

The historical market is massive and hungry. Good research is essential to communicate the feel of the period without making mistakes. Sensuality levels vary from the chaste to the explicit. (Harlequin Historicals, Harlequin Regency, Zebra Historicals, Signet Regencies)

6. Inspirational

Inspirational romances portray characters with strong religious convictions. If you are not familiar with this genre and wish to explore it, look for romances in a Christian bookstore. (Questar Publishers, Tyndale House Publishers Inc.)

b. Publishers' addresses

Below are some of the major publishers in the romance field. For a more complete list, refer to sources listed under *Annually Updated Market Information* in Appendix 3.

Bantam Books
(Bantam Fanfare and Loveswept)
1540 Broadway
New York, NY 10036

Harlequin Mills & Boon Ltd.
(Harlequin Romances and Presents,
Mills & Boon Romances)
Eton House, 18-24 Paradise Road
Richmond, Surrey
TW9 ISR   UK

Harlequin Books (Canada)
(Harlequin Love and Laughter, Regency,
Temptation, Superromance)
225 Duncan Mill Road
Don Mills, ON M3B 3K9

Harlequin Books
(Harlequin American, Historicals,
and Intrigue)
300 East 42nd Street, 6th Floor
New York, NY 10017

Kensington Publishing Corporation
(Zebra/Kensington/Pinnacle/Z-Fave)
850 3rd Avenue
New York, NY 10022

Silhouette Books
(Silhouette Intimate Moments, Romance,
and Special Edition)
300 East 42nd Street, 6th Floor
New York, NY 10017

Appendix 3
Resources

a. Romance Writers of America

The largest romance writers group in the world, Romance Writers of America (RWA), has members in many countries and over 100 affiliated chapters. Members receive a bimonthly magazine with information on markets, contests, and conferences, and articles by other writers. Members are eligible to enter the Golden Heart contest for unpublished writers. Awards are given at the RWA national conference attended each year by published and unpublished writers from around the world, by editors from all major romance publishing houses, and by many literary agents. RWA publishes an *Agent Handbook* and a *Rate the Publishers Survey.* Local chapters of RWA have regular meetings, often offering workshops by member authors. Contact:

> RWA Headquarters
> 13700 Veterans Memorial, Suite 315
> Houston, TX 77014
> Phone: (713) 440-6885

b. Courses and seminars

Dogwood Technical Services Inc. offers seminars on audio tape by Vanessa Grant and other authors and live seminars by arrangement. Call 1-800-667-6446 for a free catalogue, or visit on the Internet — http://www.islandnet.com/~dtsi/romance.htm

Writer's Digest School offers courses for writers, including Elements of Effective Writing, a course designed to improve grammar and composition skills. Contact:

Writer's Digest School
Attn: Registrar
1507 Dana Avenue
Cincinnati, OH 45207
Phone: 1-800-759-0963
Outside the U.S.A.: (513) 531-2690, extension 342

c. Software, templates, and macros

Impact Software offers *Almanac,* a personal organizer with built-in almanac of sunrise/sunset and moonrise/moonset for many worldwide locations. Ability to add any location for which you have longitude and latitude. Contact:

Impact Software
P.O. Box 457
Chino, CA 91708-0457

Dogwood Technical Services Inc. has a variety of writer's software, templates, and macros, including the following:

- *Dogwood Compendium of Names* is a 29,000 name electronic database of character names. Designed for writers, the compendium can be searched by meaning, ethnic origin, or name. Names can be searched for names that "begin with," "end with," or "contain" certain letters. For Windows 3.1 and Windows 95.

- *Literary Project Tracker* is an electronic marketing database for writers. Keep track of writing projects, submissions, letters to publishers, and follow-ups. For Windows 3.1 and Windows 95.

- *Templates and Macros for Writers* is a collection of word processor templates including Vanessa Grant's book notes templates, templates for long documents, and macros for highlighting problem words and phrases in revisions. Available for Lotus Amipro, Corel Word Perfect, and Microsoft Word for Windows. Contact:

Dogwood Technical Services Inc.
Box 8
Gabriola, BC V0R 1X0
Phone: 1-800-667-6446

Outside North America: (250) 754-1317
E-mail: dtsi@islandnet.com
Internet: http://www.islandnet.com/~dtsi/

d. Internet sites and services

Sites and services on the Internet are constantly changing. The following are World Wide Web sites which have regularly updated links to other writers' sites. For more sites, try using your Internet browser, clicking on "Net Search" and searching for "romance writing."

- *Amazon Books*, the world's largest bookstore, offers customers the ability to search from over one million titles on-line and to order books for delivery anywhere in the world. Located at — http://www.amazon.com

- *BDD Romance Forum* is Bantam/Doubleday/Dell's romance home page with information on current Loveswept romances, authors, and submissions. Located at — http://www.bdd.com/romance

- *Canadian Romance Authors Network* (CRAN) maintains a home page with information on Canadian Romance Authors and CRAN, links to authors and publishers' sites, and a bulletin board for posting notices or questions. Located at — http://www.islandnet.com/~dtsi/cran.htm

- *Dogwood Writers Page* has links to research sources, publishers, writers, software for writers, and romance writing seminars on tape. Located at — http://www.islandnet.com/~dtsi/writer.htm

- *Vanessa Grant* maintains a home page with information about her books and upcoming seminars. Located at — http://www.islandnet.com/~dtsi/vgrant.htm

- *Harlequin Enterprises Web Site* with current Harlequin, Silhouette, Mira releases, and author links. Located at — http://www.Romance.net/

- *Novelists Inc* maintains a home page dedicated to its purpose of serving the needs of multi-published writers of popular fiction. Located at — http://www.ninc.com

- *Romance Novel Database* has listings for romance novels by title, author, genre, and ratings. Links to many authors' Web pages

and other romance sites. Located at —
http://www.sils.umich.edu/~sooty/romance/

- *Romance Writers of America* home page has information on RWA membership, awards information, bestsellers information, links to writers and publishers home pages, and links to RWA individual chapter home pages. Located at — http://www.rwanational.com

- *The Romance Writer's Reference Page*: Manderley catalogue of Romance Writer's reference books. Located at — http://www.sodacreekpress.com/Romance_Ref.html

- *RW-L* is a free romance writers mailing list you can use to learn about the genre, ask your writing questions, and read answers from published and unpublished writers. To sign up, send a one line e-mail message with the contents **subRW-L<Your first and last name>** to — listserv@cornell.edu

e. *Annually updated market information*

Guide to Literary Agents. Edited by Kirsten C. Holm. Cincinnati: Writer's Digest Books.

Romance Writer's Pink Pages. Edited by Eve Paludan. Rocklin: Prima Publishing. (P.O. Box 1260, Rocklin, CA 95677. Phone: (916) 632-4400. Includes many publishers' guidelines and editors and agents' names and addresses.)

The Writer's Handbook. Edited by Sylvia K. Burack. Boston: The Writer Inc. (120 Boylston Street, Boston, MA 02116-4615. Market information plus many excellent articles on writing.)

Writer's Market. Edited by Mark Garvey. Cincinnati: Writer's Digest Books.

f. *A select bibliography*

Several of the books listed below are published by Writer's Digest Books. See *Writer's Digest* magazine for notices of new releases. Books can be ordered from:

Writer's Digest Books
1507 Dana Avenue
Cincinnati, OH 45207
Phone 1-800-289-0963

Berne, Eric. *Games People Play*. New York: Grove Press, 1964.

Bickham, Jack M. *The 38 Most Common Fiction Writing Mistakes and How to Avoid Them*. Cincinnati: Writer's Digest Books, 1992.

———. *Scene and Structure: How to construct fiction with scene-by-scene flow, logic and readability*. Cincinnati: Writer's Digest Books, 1993.
Bickham explains the flow of a story better than anyone I know.

———. *Writing Novels that Sell*. New York: Simon and Schuster, 1989.
A very readable book on the basics of developing a novel. Good resource for viewpoint, pacing, and story development.

Block, Lawrence. *Spider, Spin Me A Web: Lawrence Block on Writing Fiction*. Cincinnati: Writer's Digest Books, 1988.
Storytelling advice from a bestselling award-winning author. Block is readable, humorous, and helpful.

———. *Telling Lies for Fun and Profit*. New York: Arbor House, 1981.
A compilation of Block's articles about everything from character building to handling rejection.

Browne, Renni, and Dave King. *Self Editing for Fiction Writers: How to Edit Yourself Into Print*. New York: HarperCollins, 1993.
Good guidance in developing a professional polish to your writing. Good explanation of viewpoint, showing, and telling.

Cameron, Julia. *The Artist's Way: A Spiritual Path to Higher Creativity*. New York: Putnam, 1992.
This powerful book could change your life; certainly it will free some of your creative abilities. Wonderful guidance for seeking and using good criticism and defending from destructive criticism.

Cheney, Theodore A. Rees. *Getting the Words Right: How to Rewrite, Edit and Revise*. Cincinnati: Writer's Digest Books, 1983.

Clark, Thomas et al. *Writer's Digest Guide to Good Writing*. Cincinnati: Writer's Digest Books, 1994.
A compilation of the best of 75 years of *Writer's Digest* magazine articles about writing. Includes articles by Jude Deveraux, Isaac Asimov, Orson Scott Card, Lawrence Block, and Stephen King.

Estes, Clarissa Pinkola. *Women Who Run With the Wolves: Myths and Stories of the Wild Woman Archetype*. New York: Ballantine Books, 1992.
A thorough examination of this archetype which fits many bestselling romantic heroines.

Fast, Julius. *Body Language*. New York: Pocket Books, 1971.

Fiske, Robert Hartwell. *Thesaurus of Alternatives to Worn-Out Words and Phrases*. Cincinnati: Writer's Digest Books, 1994.

Goldberg, Natalie. *Writing Down the Bones: Freeing the Writer Within*. Boston: Shambahla Publications, 1986.
Wonderful suggestions for how to get the words flowing.

Gray, John. *Men are from Mars, Women are from Venus*. New York: HarperCollins, 1992.
Good resource for understanding how speech and motivation of men and women differ.

Grescoe, Paul. *The Merchants of Venus: Inside Harlequin and the Empire of Romance*. Vancouver: Raincoast Books, 1996.
An examination of Harlequin's domination of the romance industry based on interviews with writers, readers, employees, and ex-employees of Harlequin.

Jensen, Margaret Ann. *Love's $weet Return: The Harlequin Story*. Toronto: Women's Educational Press, 1984.
Examination of Harlequin's success and how the content of romances has changed with women's roles in society.

Krentz, Jayne Ann. *Dangerous Men and Adventurous Women: Romance Writers on the Appeal of Romance*. Philadelphia: University of Pennsylvania Press, 1992.
Excellent exploration of why romance novels have such enduring appeal.

Lamott, Anne. *Bird by Bird: Some Instructions on Writing and Life*. New York: Pantheon Books, 1994.
Great for lifting your spirits in moments when you feel discouraged as a writer.

Macauley, Robie, and George Lanning. *Technique in Fiction*. New York: St. Martin's Press, 1987.
A classic writer's resource including guidelines on style, characterization, point of view, setting, plot, pacing, and story.

New York Public Library and The Stonesong Press. *The New York Public Library Writer's Guide to Style and Usage*. New York: HarperCollins, 1994.

Pianka, Phyllis Taylor. *How to Write Romances*. Cincinnati: Writer's Digest Books, 1988.

Provost, Gary. *Make Your Words Work: Proven Techniques for Effective Writing*. Cincinnati: Writer's Digest Books, 1990.

Seger, Linda. *Creating Unforgettable Characters.* New York: Henry Holt, 1990.

Strunk, William and E.B. White. *The Elements of Style.* New York: Macmillan, 1959.

This little book, reissued many times and recommended by many writing experts, contains every basic principle of good writing style.

Swain, Dwight V. *Techniques of the Selling Writer.* Norman: University of Oklahoma Press, 1965.

Classic compilation of plotting and writing skills used in many creative writing courses.

Vogler, Christopher. *The Writer's Journey: Mythic Structure for Storytellers and Screenwriters.* Studio City: Michael Wiese Productions, 1992.

A fascinating examination of the archetypes that underlie fictional characters and plots.

Index

Page references in bold refer to illustrations.

If you have enjoyed this book and would like to receive a free catalogue of all Self-Counsel titles, please write to the appropriate address below:

Self-Counsel Press
1481 Charlotte Road
North Vancouver, B.C.   V7J 1H1

Self-Counsel Press
1704 N. State Street
Bellingham, WA   98225

Or visit us on the World Wide Web at *http://www.self-counsel.com/*